"... a great eye-opener for those who find no time for themselves. *Finding Rest When the Work Is Never Done* is a reawakening of the need for a Sabbath day in every life as well as a look at God's plan for our health. Patrick has some good insights for the Christian about how to deal with the cultural mindset of living at full speed (open throttle)."

Phil Downer
President, Christian Business Men's Committee
Ministry to the Marketplace

Finding Rest

When the Work Is Never Done

PATRICK KLINGAMAN

Cook Communications

Victor is an imprint of
Cook Communications Ministries, Colorado Springs,
Colorado 80918
Cook Communications, Paris, Ontario
Kingsway Communications, Eastbourne, England

Cover and Interior Design: RJS Design
Cover Photo: Stephanie Rausser
Editor: Greg Clouse

CIP data applied for

Table of Contents

To God, who has put so many companions in my life's path
to love and encourage me, especially Jesus, His Son,
and Kathy, my wife and best friend.

Part I: Living in a Restless World

Our culture moves at such a breathless pace that, for many, the mere thought of rest is a pipe dream. Who has time for rest anymore? People everywhere seem to be doing more and more, yet falling further and further behind.

This wasn't the world promised to me in my youth.

Up until I entered college, I heard about the coming "leisure" society. Increases in worker productivity would bring about a gradual reduction in the length of time we would need to work. By the turn of the century, you and I might be required to work only twenty to thirty hours a week, or so we were told.

What would we do with all this free time? We would have time to read, take classes, pursue the arts. Community problems would be solved because so many more people would volunteer their time to good causes.

This is the future we were told to expect at the dawn of the twenty-first century.

Instead, the current U.S. workforce generally spends more hours on the job than their parents did before them. Those household labor-saving devices seem to save less time than it took to earn the money to pay for them. Many complain that they don't have time to read anymore, which is particularly disturbing news to those of us who enjoy writing. Worse yet, even the most committed Christians I know say they have trouble finding time for God each day in their jam-packed schedules.

This stressful, restless world we live in might be easier to take if not for the fact that it wasn't supposed to be this way. It's as if we went out for a night on the town, expecting a leisurely eight-course gourmet feast, and instead found ourselves motoring through a fast-food drive-up window.

What happened?

Part 1 will briefly answer that question, exploring the wide range of cultur-al attitudes toward rest and how they differ dramatically from what the Bible teaches. This section also outlines the problems associated with lack of rest, showing how fatigue impacts our daily lives, including our walk with God and our service to Him.

Chapter 1

Is It Normal to Be So Tired?

Walter poured another cup of coffee for his friend Don, and leaned back in his heavy cedar rocker. "Beautiful morning, isn't it?"

Don nodded. "Perfect porch-sittin' weather, it is." They both smiled and turned their faces toward the sun that cut the spring morning chill.

"Isn't that the Jones fella?" Walter pointed at the big blue sedan racing past.

"I think so. We don't normally get out here in time to see him leave for work. He must be running a little late." One by one they watched as each house on the block emptied of its occupants, who quickly rushed into vehicles and sped away. Several households didn't even take the time to scoop the morning newspaper off the front porch.

"Well, Walt, did we ever move that fast in our day?"

During the toughest financial times, Walter could remember holding a couple jobs to keep a roof over his family's head. But no, he couldn't remember ever moving that fast. "The funny thing is that they never slow down. Leave early for work, stay late, shuffle the children all over town, fix up the house."

"Yeah, you're right. People don't even slow down on Sundays anymore.

All the stores stay open. Just another workday."

Walter chuckled. Since his not-so-voluntary early retirement, every day seemed like Sunday to him. All those tired-looking people and here he had all the time in the world for rest and relaxation. He felt a little guilty, but a sip of steaming coffee and a survey of the rainbow of spring flowers in the neighborhood helped him get over it.

A poke in the arm from Don jolted him out of his daydream. "Why do you think they keep building big front porches on so many of the new houses these days?"

"What are you talking about?" Walter was sure his friend had reached his coffee limit and his mind was wandering.

"All these big porches around. Ever see anyone sitting on them?"

"Just sitting?"

"Yeah."

Walter leaned back and thought about the many beautiful days he had enjoyed from his own front porch. So many glorious days, and yet all the other porches in the neighborhood were empty. Everyone else was too busy to sit.

We live in a culture that seems to move at the speed of light and never stops, making front porches wasted space.

I don't think anyone needs to be convinced that our world and the people in it move faster than anyone in the history of this planet. Accelerating technology is just one factor that has helped make blinding change the norm. Trying to keep up with those changes leaves us breathlessly running through life at an all-out sprint.

At this moment in our history when we most desperately need to rest, it is difficult to even slow down a little, much less pause for rest.

I need to start out by confessing that it has not long been my ambition to write a book about rest. My primary area of teaching and writing has been to help people develop a biblical perspective on work; that is, to make their work part of their service to God. What could be further from rest than that?

In my research on the topic of work, I saw how sin causes people to either worship work or abhor it. To help people avoid those sins, I felt that I needed to season my teaching on the value of work with some biblical instruction on rest. As a result, I included a session on rest in my ten-week "Thank God It's Monday" adult Sunday School series, plus a chapter on avoiding work addiction in my book of the same title.

I was not fully prepared for the response the first time I taught about rest. It was if I had opened the floodgates of emotions in the class. People shared how they were overcommitted, overwhelmed, and unsure of how to slow down the pace of life enough to catch their breath. It took us two weeks to cover that single lesson on rest—and we could have gone further if we didn't have a schedule to keep (how ironic!).

Five years later, I expanded my rest curriculum to nearly eight hours of material in order to teach an adult elective at a church vacation Bible school. As I pulled together my biblical research, I was astounded at how the topic of rest cuts to the heart of our relationship with God, covering issues like anxiety, contentment, and our prayer life. When I saw how God's Word changed people's lives during the week of classes, I knew I could no longer put off writing this book.

Even though rest is present right from Day 7 of the Creation account, it doesn't seem to attract as much attention as other biblical topics. I used to think work was an undertaught topic until I tried to remember ever hearing a sermon on rest. I recall one "keeping the Sabbath holy" sermon, but its main point was to convince people they needed to be in church. It appears that teaching on rest is in as short supply as rest itself.

Attitudes Toward Rest

When we don't have proper biblical instruction on a topic, improper attitudes and practices can develop. In a world obsessed with activity, it is easy to feel its influence. For example, which of the following best describes your dominant view on rest?

• **Rest is evil.** Many people take literally the phrase, "Idleness is the devil's workshop." Of course the Bible doesn't actually teach that rest is wicked, but that the wicked never rest. Big difference.

• **Rest is okay for certain weak people, but not for me.** Those addicted to work often see rest as something only for the weak, for losers. "Winners" can't afford such nonproductive activity. Part of their edge is working harder and longer than those they compete against.

• **I rest only when I need to (or when I am forced to).** This attitude reflects the influence of utilitarianism, which suggests that rest is good only if it makes us more productive and more useful in the long run. For years I rested only when my body or mind told me I was too tired to go on.

• **I've tried to rest, but I feel too guilty about it.** Many of us sense the need for rest, but feel guilty forgoing productive activity in order to restore ourselves. As a result, our attempts to rest are futile and frustrating.

• **I rest only when I finish all my work.** For many, this is a carryover from childhood, when our parents would let us go out to play only after we finished all our homework. As adults, however, our "homework" is rarely ever done. This view of rest as extra or free time has contributed to its decline as people's schedules get more crowded.

• **I should rest more, but just can't find the time.** Most of us are passive in scheduling our time, so work and social/family obligations tend to dominate what we put on our calendars. Without sound management, these items can become the sum total of our day-to-day existence. Since we never make a rest appointment, it never happens.

• **I value rest and usually get enough.** Some people do a good job of resting during their normal schedule, but struggle to maintain it during "crunch" times. Unfortunately, crunch time is when rest is needed most. As a result, we often experience some form of a "crash" after our crisis is over.

• **I regularly schedule the rest I need.** The consistently rested individual is a rare being in our culture. This is a person who seems to have deep reserves of energy and accomplishes much, yet rarely appears rushed. He or she has a strong, quiet spirit that reminds us of how Jesus lived His life on earth.

Potential Problems with Lack of Rest

Although many of us have been influenced by some of the worldly views on rest, most of us will readily admit that we desire and need more rest than we get. Still, the treadmill of life seems to speed up every year so, despite our good intentions, we don't take steps to correct the problem.

In my own case, I felt a twinge of guilt every time I read about the Sabbath regulations in the Old Testament. Even though God commanded a day of rest dedicated to Him, I did little more than slow down a little on Sundays. My sleep habits were marginal, as I limited myself to the absolute minimum "snooze" time necessary to function. And even though Jesus advised the weary to come to Him, I was very erratic and sporadic in my prayer life. I knew I should do these things, but life was just so hectic.

My behavior changed little until I began to ponder the value of rest. Actually, the value of rest was made most clear to me as I discovered the impact of lack of rest. God designed us to need rest; ignoring that need brings about disastrous consequences:

• **Poor health.** Two-thirds of physician office visits are said to be stress related. The nonstop, frantic pace of our culture has coincided with an increase in ailments as minor as headaches, to major illnesses like depression and heart disease. We will discuss the physical impact of lack of rest in greater detail in chapter 3.

• **Decline in quality (and perhaps quantity) of life.** Stopping to smell the roses or whatever else brings us joy is an important part of living a full life. Life in a rush often doesn't give us time to feel the joy of what we are doing. Also, physicians and other medical experts are finding that high-stress people who are always on the go may be cutting their lives short because of their lifestyles. It is ironic that in our rush to do more we may actually accomplish less.

• **We make work an idol.** When we can't stand a moment without doing something productive, we need to address the possibility that we are addicted to work. If our compulsion to work is greater than our desire to obey God, work has become an idol. The importance of rest to God will be discussed in greater detail in chapter 2.

• **Family strain.** When I am under extreme time pressure, I find that I am more irritable and may resent time spent with other people. Our spouses, our children, and other family members become another obligation on our list instead of a source of joy and thanksgiving. Strong relationships take time to build and maintain. Restless people in an endless cycle of activity often don't or can't make that kind of commitment.

• **Less time for God.** I find it ironic that so often, when I am most in need of God's strength and wisdom, I am most inconsistent in my time with Him. If we desire to commit our lives to God and serve Him, significant daily time in prayer and Scripture reading is without a doubt our most important activity. By not slowing down to be with God, we avoid an important daily rest provision with which God has blessed us.

• **Less reflection on direction and decisions.** Ever notice how difficult it is to stay thoughtful and prayerful in the midst of our daily battles? Constant activity keeps our brains too busy to quietly mull over life's decisions or the direction we are heading. Proverbs 19:2 warns us not "to be hasty and miss the way," while Proverbs 14:8 notes, "The wisdom of the prudent is to give thought to their ways." Quiet reflection, combined with prayerful petition, is essential to stay on course in the world in which we live. Nearly all of the decisions that I have regretted in my life have been made in a hurry or without thoughtful consideration.

• **Our witness is weakened.** As Christians, we have the opportunity to stand out in a hurried, harried world. When we are "just like everyone else," those in the world have difficulty seeing the impact of Jesus in our lives. Imagine the impact of the calm presence of Jesus if He were to suddenly appear on the floor of the New York Stock Exchange in the middle of heated trading. Would He be noticed? I think so! With Jesus in our hearts, our potential to stand out in our own world is just as dramatic. When we lack rest and suffer the consequences, we hinder the ability of our light to shine before the lost.

• **We miss or dismiss God-given opportunities.** God desires for each one of us to participate in His work as members of the body of Christ. That work might be involvement in a church ministry or involvement in the lives of the lost and misguided we come across each day. When our schedules have no time for new projects—no extra time to pause, ponder, and pray—then it is difficult to notice the daily opportunities for ministry God sends our way. Even if we did notice, when would we have time to do them? We become like those who rushed past the wounded traveler at the roadside instead of like the Samaritan who took the time to care.

I was a runner for a good portion of my life, until one of my knees decided that it strongly preferred me to walk instead. Even when I was well conditioned, I found that my body began to wane after about five or six miles of running—not even an hour of effort. If you want to see what several hours of running does to the body, spend some time hanging around the finish line of a marathon. It isn't pretty.

In our fast-paced culture, trying to live without rest is like trying to sprint through a marathon. Life becomes a weary struggle for survival instead of a gift to enjoy. In my case, I have ignored every biblical principle regarding rest and have faced many of the consequences we just covered. As God began to teach me the spiritual value of rest from His Word and through prayer, I have started the journey from being "restless" to "rested." In chapter 2 we will begin to examine God's view of rest, exploring the biblical relationship between work and rest.

Next Step

Think about your own attitudes toward rest. Of the attitudes listed in the chapter, which best describes how you feel and act? Take a few minutes to explore the reasons why you feel the way you do about rest. If you don't feel you are getting enough rest, make a list of the reasons why.

Chapter 2

Created for Both Work and Rest

It wasn't until afternoon that I could start my annual garden-planting day. I had stared impatiently out the window all morning as a steady shower soaked both of my tilled but barren garden beds.

Normally I like to see it rain, especially in the spring. Today I grumbled about how April showers couldn't bring May flowers if the plants were still sitting in my garage.

Finally, the dark clouds passed and I was freed from my indoor pacing. When the dirt from the first hole stuck stubbornly to my shovel, I sensed that my planting day might have to be completed under moonlight. I would get it done, though, no matter what. I tried to apply my business training to the task, digging multiple holes before tossing aside the shovel and setting the plants in their new muddy home.

My back ached as I tilled the last of the smooth soil of the first garden bed. Why did I buy so many plants? If I had decided on a more Spartan-looking garden, I'd be done by now. But no, this year I was determined to make the Tournament of Roses parade look colorless by comparison.

One garden was now planted; now my eyes were fixed on the bare plot on *the other side of the yard. My mouth was dry, so I decided to grab a can of soda on my way to the garage to pick up more plants. As I stood before the array of bundles and pots, I glanced up and noticed the hibernating lawn chairs hanging from nails along the wall. I grabed a chair instead of more plants; I just didn't want to bend over again yet.*

An inner great debate ensued during my brief journey to the front yard. If you plant yourself in that chair, you'll never finish by the end of the day—and you always finish in one day. But my body hurts. Gardens are a place to work, not to loaf. Aren't those dark clouds on the horizon? What if God had quit after planting just half of the Garden of Eden?

Discussion ended as I sat down overlooking the site of my afternoon's labor. For the first time, I looked back on what I had accomplished, instead of straining ahead toward the next hole to dig. Not bad. No flowers yet, of course, but the legions of little green stems were an improvement. I imagined the sea of color I would soon be enjoying as my plants came into bloom. I even thought of a way to arrange the next bed so it would look even better.

In Genesis 1, God paused seven times during His work of creation to look at what He had done and deem that it was good—and not always at the end of the day. Most days I scurry from task to task, not pausing to see if there is any good in what I do. Today, I decided not to skip the "good" part.

In our headlong dash to get stuff done, many of us seem to be missing the good part of life. It's not that work isn't good. Work is good, but compulsive, frantic, restless work that never ends is neither good nor biblical.

Up until quite recently, I thought work was the most important part of life. I also thought I had the Bible to back me up. After all, God created six times the number of work days as days of rest, right?

With my business training, I was very focused on what I thought was the bottom line: getting stuff done. As I grew as a Christian, my emphasis was still on getting stuff done, but now it was doing things for God and His kingdom. Surely God values our efforts for Him far more than "do-nothing" resting.

Our culture certainly values activity over rest. "Just Do It" could be our national slogan, not just a tag line to sell shoes. Most people I know have as their goal to accomplish and experience as much as possible, cramming all they can into their short existence on earth.

For most of my life I concentrated solely on what I was to accomplish. For me, rest was only a necessary break so I could get more done in the long run, a view I still stubbornly clung to when I started researching this book.

I was wrong. As I reread some key Bible verses on rest, God showed me just how off base my views were. Let's look at some of those passages:

• **God made the day He rested a holy day, not the six days He worked (Genesis 2:2-3).** Most of us are fairly familiar with the Creation account in the Book of Genesis. God created the material world we dwell in and then rested on the seventh day. In reading these chapters, it is easy to focus on the six days of creation work and miss the importance of the seventh. Did God bless the six days of work and make them holy? No, in Genesis 2:3 "God blessed the seventh day and made it holy" because that was the day He rested from His work. From the beginning of the world then, rest has value because God gave it value by His blessing. It is not meant to be a practical "activity" but a holy one.

• **God rested as an example for us to follow (Exodus 20:8-11).** This passage, the longest of the Ten Commandments, tells us to honor the Sabbath by keeping it holy. Keeping it holy is easy: no one in the household is to do work of any kind. These verses also help answer the question of why God rested on the seventh day. Did He need to rest? No, I doubt our omnipotent God was tired. Was His work all done? Although God had finished the initial act of creating, His work—as evidenced throughout the Bible—was far from over. Instead, He rested to set an example for us to follow. We are to work six days but rest the seventh, says verse 11, "For in six days the Lord made the heavens and the earth, the sea, and all that is in them, but he rested on the seventh day. Therefore the Lord blessed the Sabbath day and made it holy."

• **Sabbath rest was the sign that was to distinguish Israel from the other, restless nations (Exodus 31:13, 16-17).** Sometimes it is easy to dismiss Sabbath rest as just part of the Old Testament law, rules that we are "free" from through our relationship with Jesus Christ. Sabbath rest wasn't just part of the law, wasn't just one of the Ten Commandments, but a sign of the covenant between God and Israel. Exodus 31:16-17 reads, "The Israelites are to observe the Sabbath, celebrating it for the generations to come as a lasting covenant. It will be a sign between me and the Israelites forever. ...." As a branch that has been grafted onto the tree of God's chosen people, Christians should not be quick to dismiss this sign of God's covenant relationship.

• **Nothing else in life must crowd out rest (Exodus 34:21).** It is easy to put off rest until life gets a little less hectic. "I'll get some rest as soon as I finish this project," we say, yet we find other projects waiting for us when we are done with that one. Exodus 34:21 commands the Israelites to rest, "even during the plowing season and harvest." Those who grew up on a farm will not have to be reminded that the times of sowing and harvest were always the busiest of the year. People worked every available daylight hour to get the crops planted or picked. Farmers aren't the only ones who face "crunch time," times when we need to dig down deep to move the mountain of work in front of us. Still, the Bible teaches us that missing Sabbath rest is not excusable, even during crunch time.

• **Not resting was a capital offense (Exodus 35:2).** In the Old Testament law, there was no penalty for not working on a particular day. To work on the Sabbath, however, carried the most severe penalty of all: death. Think about it—working seven days a week was to bring about the same punishment as cold-blooded murder. Why? The best answer I can find is that both were acts of disobedience, violating something critically important to God. Killing a human being destroys a creature created in the image of God. Working on the Sabbath desecrates the Lord's Day, the day He made holy because He rested.

Why Don't We Rest?
If God commands us to rest and it is intended for our benefit, why don't we obey? Part of the answer to that question we discussed in the

last chapter. Teaching on rest has been minimal in the church, so many of us spend a good portion of our lives unaware of its importance to God. We might dismiss it as Old Testament legalism or figure that we are doing okay if we occasionally take a day off from the grind. If we understood the value of rest in God's eyes, we might seek it with joy instead of avoiding it.

Lack of instruction contributes to the problem, to be sure, but it hardly explains our restless culture. How is it that everything in our daily walk in the world seems to conspire against us pausing to catch our breath and regain our bearings?

In my research, I found many experts who offered clues as to why we don't rest. Tim Hansel cites utilitarianism and a suspicion of pleasure as one cause. In *When I Relax I Feel Guilty*, he writes:

> In our worthy attempt to avoid idleness and questionable pleasures, we begin to feel that everything must be useful. Thus, our false guilt compels us to read for profit, attend parties for contacts, exercise so we can work better, and rest in order to be more efficient. We regress to a kind of neopuritanism that says, "You have not been born into the world for pleasure." A curious and familiar psychological need to justify everything emerges, leaving no room for discovery and pure enjoyment. [1]

Others put different labels on our compulsion to do. Doctors Robert Hemfelt, Frank Minirth, and Paul Meier, in their book *We Are Driven* call it drivenness, which they define as "an insatiable drive to do more and be more. It's a drive that may be masked by charitable and positive motives, but in reality originates in deep, perhaps even unconscious, feelings of inadequacy and shame." [2]

Some look beyond individual traits and indict the culture we live in. Dr. Richard A. Swenson believes that societal progress has contributed to our overloaded lives by decreasing our "margin," that is, our emotional, physical, financial, and time reserves. In his book *Margin*, Swenson writes, "There can be little doubt that the ubiquitous contemporary absence of margin is directly linked to the march of progress. Those cultures with the most progress are the same as those with the least margin." [3]

Others point to more specific cultural trends that decrease rest time, such as the lengthening of the workweek and the rise of two-income families. Juliet Schor, in her 1991 book, *The Overworked American*, claims that the amount of time Americans spend working has steadily increased during the past twenty years—adding the equivalent of an extra day or more of work each year. Her explanation for the increase in hours worked includes the unchecked greed of many employers plus a stronger materialistic desire in American families. [4]

Of course we are still only scratching the service in terms of culprits for our restlessness. Yet each of these explanations, if we dig around the base of them, shares a common root cause: sin. This problem goes a lot deeper than not resting on the Sabbath. Restlessness is not merely a by-product of stress, but a warning sign that something is missing in our relationship to God.

Sound a little far-fetched? Not if you look through the Bible closely. Rest, both individually and collectively, has always been considered a trait of one whose relationship to God is strong. When the nation of Israel was walking right with their Lord, Scripture gives frequent references to God giving their land rest—meaning they were at peace with each other and with neighboring nations. Notice how God describes Solomon and his kingdom in 1 Chronicles 22:9, a passage where God tells King David that his son will build God's temple. "But you will have a son who will be a man of peace and rest, and I will give him rest from all his enemies on every side. His name will be Solomon, and I will grant Israel peace and quiet during his reign."

Of course, when Israel drifted from God, peace and rest disappeared, replaced by war and a host of other restless pursuits. Unfortunately, the situation for God's chosen people had to become fearfully desperate before they would turn back to God, but when they did, He delivered them and restored peace to the land.

Individuals, too, lack peace when they live apart from God. In Isaiah 57:20-21, the wicked are likened to "the tossing sea, which cannot rest whose waves cast up mire and mud. 'There is no peace,' says my God, 'for the wicked.'" A tossing sea is the perfect description of my mind when I am overcome with anxiety or anger or hurt over a particular situation—until I come on my knees to the God of Peace.

When we turn to God, He gives us rest and peace. In Psalm 62:1, David proclaims, "My soul finds rest in God alone." Also, Jesus promises rest for those who seek Him: "Come to me, all you who are weary and burdened, and I will give you rest. Take my yoke upon you and learn from me, for I am gentle and humble in heart, and you will find rest for your souls. For my yoke is easy and my burden is light" (Matthew 11:28).

Notice how the promises of Christ contrast with what the world offers. Christ promises rest while the world offers endless pursuits and diversions. Christ teaches us to replace our burdens with His lighter yoke; the world tells us that it is all up to us. When we follow Christ, we fall in step with a gentle and humble Leader who, during His walk on earth, never appeared to be in a hurry. When we hop on the world's bandwagon, we find life to be hurried and harsh.

We live in an impatient world that wants instant satisfaction, yet we serve a patient, enduring, eternal God. This dramatic contrast makes it easier for us to determine which has the greatest influence on our lives. According to Tim Kimmel in *Little House on the Freeway*, hurry and impatience come from the influence of sin:

> Our hurried lifestyle is a result of taking shortcuts in life. Since the fall of man in the Garden of Eden, sin has refused to let us rest. Stripped to its core, sin is "the desire to have it now." Sin is the enemy of time. It takes time to be organized. It takes time to mean-ingfully communicate. It takes time to develop intimate friend-ships. It takes time to build character in a child. Warped by sin, our egos look for cheap shortcuts. Instead, we end up restless and dis-satisfied with life. [5]

Restlessness and hurry are by-products of sin, but their real danger is that they preempt reflection and meaningful time with God. Psalm 46:10 states, "Be still, and know that I am God." I think the wisdom of that verse is lost on our culture. Being still must happen in order for us to fully feel the presence of God and hear His voice. We need to take our minds off our worldly pursuits for awhile so we can focus on God. We need to pause from our doing to consider who God is and who we are in Christ. We also need to wait expectantly on our Lord to guide us in the direction we should go and grow next.

Unfortunately, some illustrations that are used to discourage idleness can encourage restlessness. Many times I have heard the expression that it is easier to steer a vehicle when it is moving than when it is standing still. his adage is aimed at the idle person who says he is waiting for direction, but doing nothing in the meantime. In work, for instance, sometimes we need to try a new task to determine whether that might be God's will for us.

Although the moving vehicle illustration has some wisdom, it is easy to use it to justify being in constant motion, always busy. But think about it: Can you refuel a car when it is moving? Can you repair or upgrade it without stopping? Can you ask for directions without pulling off the road? A vehicle in constant motion will eventually break down or run out of gas.

Most people in our culture look up to the person who is always on the go, always doing, always achieving. God isn't quite so impressed, however, for He knows that the person who never stops never grows.

God, in His infinite wisdom, knows that we need to pause to refuel and retool for our battles in the world. The abundant life He promises us in Scripture is not the same as the hurried, jam-packed lives so many of us lead, teetering on the verge of exhaustion. He does not want us just to survive our time in this world, but to thrive. He has made provision for overcoming the weariness of life, offering rest for the body, mind, heart, and soul. The next part of this book will take a look at these four types of rest and how we can find them in the midst of our busy schedules.

Next Step

Instead of moving on to the next chapter, stop what you are doing and spend the next half hour or so thinking about your life and your walk with God. Ask yourself, "Why does God want me to rest?" Reflect on the verses presented in the chapter. Think about how faithfully observing

God's teaching on rest could impact your life. If that thinking turns to prayer, let it happen.

Notes:

1. Tim Hansel, *When I Relax I Feel Guilty* (Colorado Springs: Chariot Victor Publishing, 1979), p. 12.

2. Dr. Robert Hemfelt, Dr. Frank Minirth, and Dr. Paul Meier, *We Are Driven* (Carmel, New York: Guideposts, 1991), p. 6.

3. Richard A. Swenson, M.D., *Margin* (Colorado Springs: NavPress, 1992), p. 30.

4. Juliet B. Schor, *The Overworked American* (New York: BasicBooks, 1991), p. 1.

5. Tim Kimmel, *Little House on the Freeway* (Portland, Oregon: Multnomah Press, 1987), pp. 32-33.

Part II:
Key Components of Total Rest

Jesus taught us to "love the Lord your God with all your heart and with all your soul and with all your mind and with all your strength" (Mark 12:30). In this, the Great Commandment, we learn that there are four aspects to our love for God. We are to love Him with all our strength, meaning, in part, that we are to honor God with our bodies and make them instruments of righteousness. We must also love God with all our minds, holding every thought captive to Him and seeking to have the mind of Christ develop in us. Also, we must allow God to create in us a pure heart, a heart that controls our thoughts and actions according to God's will. Finally, we are to love Him with all our soul. Although the soul is harder to visualize than the other three, the intent of this passage is that we are to love God with all of our being, with all that we are.

Each of these aspects of our love for God is also provided for us in terms of God's rest. Since these are the four means by which we love and serve God, He has provided resources for us to draw upon in each case. The four chapters in this section will examine rest for the body, mind, heart, and soul.

Chapter 3

A Body
That Will Quit

As our plane landed at Shannon Airport in Ireland, Kathy and I had just experienced our shortest night ever. It was after 8 P.M. when we boarded our flight in Boston and 7 A.M. when we landed again, all but five hours of that was "lost" in time zone changes. Since I have great difficulty sleeping on airplanes, I walked through the airport feeling as if it were well past my bedtime, while all around me people were starting a new day.

Fortunately, we were able to check in early at our hotel by the airport. We closed the curtains and forced ourselves to take an hour nap. After a little sleep and a shower, we felt ready to start our vacation adventure. The drive to the nearby town of Ennis was uneventful, although driving on the left side of the road took some getting used to. We stopped at the local tourist office to get a town map and information on the walking tour we had read about. The ladies in the office recommended a place to start that offered free parking.

After a couple wrong turns, we found the part of town we were looking for. The parking lot sign had the name of a hotel on it, but it was a large, mostly empty lot so we parked there. When we finished our lunch and walking *tour, we returned to the car and found a parking ticket with a hefty fine, about twenty-five U.S. dollars. We looked around and discovered two large signs with clear payment instructions that we hadn't noticed on our arrival. Kathy and I also noticed the lot where we were supposed to have parked, clearly marked, just fifty yards away.*

We couldn't figure out where we needed to go to pay our ticket, so we backtracked to the tourist office where we started. Even though we had been on these roads before, we still made wrong turns before reaching our guides. They gave us clear directions and even marked our destination on a map. We still had to ask directions of nearby pedestrians more than once. Despite the extra help, it took us half an hour to find the building, after driving by it at least three or four times.

By the time we returned to our hotel, we were exhausted. We even had trouble deciding what to do about dinner, though our choices were not overwhelming. Finally we shuffled into the hotel restaurant, where we sat lifeless, waiting for our meal to arrive.

The next day had many more driving and exploring challenges, but this time we each had a long night's sleep. We were much more skilled at finding our way around, even though we had the same maps and not much more experience on Ireland's roads. When we did take a wrong turn, it was a much less frustrating setback. At the end of our second day, we were tired, but nothing like the night before.

The first day of vacation went nearly as badly as it could go, while the second was one of the best days of sightseeing my wife and I have ever had. The main difference in the two days was the degree to which our bodies had experienced rest.

Physical rest—that is, rest for the body—seems so basic and obvious, yet it is surprising how little most people get. We tend to take our bodies for granted until we face more extreme circumstances, like a night without sleep, an illness, or even complete physical exhaustion.

Before completing research for this book, I would not have considered physical rest nearly as important as rest for the mind, heart, and soul. After all, God is a spiritual being more concerned with spiritual matters than fleshly ones.

I was wrong. As Christians we tend to emphasize the spiritual aspects of our Sunday Sabbaths, since that is the day we usually come together for worship in church. Interestingly, worship is not emphasized in the Old Testament Sabbath passages; only the ceasing of work. God's people were repeatedly instructed to set aside their physical labors for a day each week. Neither they nor their servants nor their animals were to perform work of any kind. This was central to the Sabbath commandment.

God knew from the beginning that people would be prone to wearing themselves out trying to cram two or three lifetimes of activity into one. He understands better than we do the importance of regularly coming to a complete halt before beginning another week of activity.

Our culture differs from biblical times in that our labors are often more mental than physical. Yet, as we will see later, the health of mind and body are tightly intertwined. No matter how mental our work may be, once our bodies go, our ability to get work done is gone. According to Stephen Covey and Roger and Rebecca Merrill, "Our body is a fundamental stewardship; it's the instrument through which we work to fulfill all other stewardships and responsibilities." [1]

Physical Implications of Lack of Rest

I worked in the health-care field for more than eleven years and saw firsthand the consequence of ignoring the needs of our bodies. Heart attacks, strokes, sleep problems, weight problems, chronic fatigue syndrome, high cholesterol. The list goes on.

Hospitals used to be filled with people fighting diseases like smallpox and polio. Dr. Archibald Hart points out that people are increasingly dying from the effects of too much stress, which differs from the diseases of the past in that it is largely self-induced. [2]

Physicians like Dr. Richard Swenson note that the abuse of our bodies has changed the nature of the medical profession:

In many ways, the practice of medicine was more rewarding when patients were victimized by external tragedies than it is now when patients so often victimize themselves. As a result of this new mor-

33

bidity, the heroic nature of medical practice has all but disappeared. A romanticized past envisions doctors risking their lives by working all hours to save a community from smallpox. Today, the vision has deteriorated into business-minded physicians taking care of patients with self-induced illnesses who live self-destructive lives, who expect to get well now and threaten to sue if they don't. [3]

What has caused this disturbing rash of self-inflicted illnesses? Two key and interrelated factors create greater havoc on our bodies than in past generations: chronic stress and inadequate sleep.

Stress That Can Kill

The human body is an amazing machine. When we face danger or a crisis, our bodies create more adrenaline so they can effectively rise up to deal with the situation. Whether it be to flee from an angry grizzly bear or to cram for an exam, our bodies respond similarly in terms of adrenaline levels and temporary increases in performance. When the crisis or danger has passed, adrenaline levels return to normal and we often experience fatigue from the physical and/or emotional stress we have experienced.

In today's culture, an increasing number of people are experiencing what seems like a never-ending cycle of stress. Many are so busy, doing so many things, that they feel they are always running behind schedule, always in a hurry. The effect of all this rushing about is to put their bodies in an almost constant state of crisis.

This continuing state of crisis is damaging to our bodies, particularly over the long haul. The adrenaline produced by a brief period of stress is not normally dangerous. When stress becomes a way of life, however, it produces a chronic increased flow of adrenaline. This can lead to dangerous physical problems such as increases in cholesterol, narrowing of blood vessels, and more plaque deposits on the walls of arteries. [4]

Dr. Archibald Hart, in his book *The Hidden Link Between Adrenalin and Stress*, also points to research suggesting that excessive stress can gradually destroy the body's immunological defense mechanisms, putting it at risk for a wide range of illnesses. He concludes that the essence of the stress problem is "we are living at a pace that is too fast for our bodies." [5]

The adage "Hard work never killed anyone" may not be entirely true. The Japanese, whose long work hours are legendary, even have a word—*karoshi*—which means "death from overwork." Karoshi may account for 10 percent of all deaths of working men in Japan. [6]

Although I have never been close to working myself to death, I have battled with overuse of adrenaline. In researching this chapter, I realized that I have relied more upon adrenaline over the years than I had thought. I did not grow up with good study habits or strong discipline— but I was impressive when faced with a deadline. I could do amazing things the day before a test or before a major project was due. Sad to say, in some courses in which I received an "A," I might have failed the final exam if it had been given to me two days beforehand.

As I have aged, my discipline has improved, but I still find myself dependent on deadline-induced adrenaline to gear up for larger projects. Wisdom has taught me to reach peak performance sooner than the day before the project is due, but I continue to rely on the looming deadline for motivation. For example, I wrote a large portion of my first book, *Thank God It's Monday*, during the final two months before the manuscript was due. It wasn't that I didn't work hard the six months before that, but the adrenaline produced by the approaching deadline allowed me to crank out pages of writing as I had never done before.

Only after the deadline pressure passed did I realize what I had done to my body and mind. I wrote my last manuscript page on Christmas Eve. That evening, while singing Christmas carols with friends, I lost my voice, which I did not regain for several days. After getting over that illness, my condition improved to mere exhaustion and "brainlessness." It took me almost a month to approach normal levels of functioning.

An ongoing high level of adrenaline is not only dangerous, it is addicting. Dr. Hart points out that the adrenaline that we depend on to "go the extra mile" produces chemical changes in the brain similar to that produced by drugs. Like the effects of drugs, we can get addicted to the rush of adrenaline. What are some warning signs that we might be dependent on adrenaline to get us through our work or other activities?

According to Dr. Hart, here are some red flags to watch for:

- You would rather engage in your activity than sleep.
- When you stop your activity you feel very unhappy.
- You feel excited or encouraged only when you engage in your activity; at other times you feel "low."
- Your activity helps you forget your problems.
- Whenever you feel depressed, you turn to your activity to make you feel better.
- You fantasize a lot about your activity when you are away from it. [7]

In Search of a Good Night's Sleep

The other cultural trend wearing out our bodies is an increasing lack of sleep. Just as deficit spending eventually bankrupts households and nations, running a sleep deficit can pose a serious danger to our bodies.

According to a 1998 survey sponsored by the National Sleep Foundation, adult Americans on average sleep just seven hours a night, significantly less than the eight to ten hours experts say we need for our bodies and minds to operate at optimal levels. Two-thirds of those surveyed reported at least one sleep-related problem, meaning sleep is a issue for most of us.

Still more disturbing is the impact of lack of sleep. According to the National Sleep Foundation survey report, 37 percent of respondents reported being so sleepy during the day that it interferes with regular activities. Twenty-three percent of adults admitted that they had actually fallen asleep while driving during the past year. [8]

Stanley Coren, professor of psychology at the University of British Columbia, says research shows that sleep levels started to decline with key technological advances during the early twentieth century. In his book *Sleep Thieves*, Coren has chronicled the plight of sleep and its troubling impact:

Despite the fact that sleep plays a vital part in our health and our efficiency, we seem out to abolish sleep. The first step in this process was the invention of the electric lightbulb, which eliminated our main excuse for stopping our work at the end of the day; namely, that it was too dark to function. Next came the continuous conveyor belt, which encouraged factories to operate 24 hours a day. Now the continuous access to information provided by the Internet and other computer communications links keeps us from our beds at all hours of the night. The work ethic we have adopted today says that we should do away with sleep, or at least eliminate as much sleep time as possible. The movers and shakers of the world don't waste their time sleeping. Yet too little sleep can kill us outright or can cause a gradual deterioration in our health. Too little sleep can make us clumsy, stupid, and accident-prone. Too little sleep can destroy our psychological motivation and put us into a deep depression. [9]

I was struck by one of the stories I read in *Sleep Thieves*. Coren, a faithful eight-hour-a-night sleeper, came across research in the early 1980s (which has since been discredited) suggesting a reasonable "sleep diet" might require only five hours a night. He was excited about the prospects of three extra hours of daily production, so he decided to reduce his sleep by a half hour a week until he reached his goal.

The journal he kept during that time told of difficulty getting out of bed, morning sluggishness, mental lapses, unplanned naps, and no motivation at the end of the day to do anything more than stare at the television screen. Instead of getting more accomplished during his longer days, both the quality and quantity of his output declined. He quit his sleep reduction efforts after just seven weeks because of the impact it was having on his body and his work.

As I read through those journal entries, I saw more of myself than I expected. Many of the disturbing effects of sleeplessness Coren experienced for the first time were old hat to me. Up until then, I thought my struggles to get up and function were normal. I did not realize that much of my clumsiness, falling asleep every other night on the sofa, and what I call my "brain dead days" could be attributed to my lack of sleep.

For years I remained more or less functional at about six hours of sleep per night. I knew my body quickly rebelled if I slept less, so six hours I slept. Still, the length of sleep had more to do with my attitudes toward work and rest than my physical requirements. For most of my adult life, I have lived with a to-do list mentality. The more things I accomplished at the end of the day, the better I felt. As bedtime approached each night, I would be faced with a choice: go to sleep at a decent time or stay up and check off one or two of the remaining items on my list.

Most nights the list won out over sleep. When I did go to bed, I almost always set my alarm for no more than six hours later, so I could get up and get productive as soon as possible. In my striving to do more, "wasting" two extra hours of potentially productive time did not seem like a fair tradeoff.

During the course of researching and writing this book, I struggled mightily to correct this obvious shortcoming in my rest needs. Over the months I slowly raised my nightly sleep average to six and a half hours, then seven hours, then seven and a half. Now I almost never fall asleep at night on the sofa and my "brain dead days" are few and far between. Plus I'm more productive during the time I am awake, which means the extra sleep time has helped, not hurt, my ability to get things done.

Sleep is not only of direct benefit to our bodies, it also helps to counter the effects of chronic stress. To avoid the damaging impact of stress-induced adrenaline, our bodies require periods of deep relaxation to allow adrenaline levels to return to normal. Sleep and other times of deep relaxation provide a counter to life's stresses and strains.

Unfortunately, for those weary with hurried, overloaded lives, sleep has somehow become an enemy instead of part of the solution. In our rush to do more, sleep is considered downtime instead of something that recharges and refreshes us. We ignore it at our own peril. Psalm 127:2 states that to rise up early and stay up late toiling in our work is in vain, for God "grants sleep to those he loves."

Running the Good Race

What would be your reaction if I knocked on your door this morning and said, "Come run a marathon with me today"?

Unless you are a well-trained runner who could call my bluff (then I would be in trouble), "no" would probably be the nicest answer I could expect to receive. After all, running 26.2 miles at one time is not something any of us would do on impulse. Without the proper preparation and training, our bodies would give out long before the finish line.

Life is like a long-distance race. The Apostle Paul uses this analogy in Acts 20:24, stating that his life is worth nothing, except that he "finish the race and complete the task the Lord Jesus has given me—the task of testifying to the gospel of God's grace." He instructs Christians in 1 Corinthians 9:24 to "run in such a way as to get the prize."

How do we run the race of life in such a way as to get the prize? Although there are many aspects to answering that question, caring for the body that takes us through the race is one aspect we often overlook. God's Word, however, provides a number of wise insights to help us keep our bodies functioning well until we reach life's finish line:

• **We are to see our bodies and treat our bodies as God's dwelling place.** Too many of us look at our bodies in a negative way, focusing on our imperfections or ways that we don't measure up to bodily standards set by our culture. How might thinking of our bodies as a temple for the Holy Spirit change the way we look at them? That is exactly how Paul describes the body in 1 Corinthians 6:19. In the next verse he concludes that because we are not our own but belong to Jesus, we should "honor God" with our bodies. It is important for us to understand that our bodies are part of our spiritual walk to be used as "instruments of righteousness" (Romans 6:13) and "living sacrifices" (Romans 12:1).

• **A weak body offsets a willing spirit.** During the night Jesus spent praying in Gethsemane just prior to His arrest, He returned to find His disciples sleeping and told them, "The spirit is willing, but the body is weak" (Matthew 26:41). His disciples had just experienced a wonderful feast with their Leader and deeply desired to stay up to pray with Him, yet after just one hour they were all fast asleep. We, too, may be filled with the desire to serve God, but when we ignore the needs of our bodies (including the need for rest), it will eventually interfere with our ability to accomplish those desires.

I once competed in a 5K run several weeks after training for and running another short race. Between races, life got hectic so I hardly trained at all. On race day I was mentally ready to run a good race, but my body reminded me within the first quarter mile that it had not been properly prepared to run at the speed I wanted to go. I finished the race, but only after being passed by a long line of runners who would not have caught me had my body been in better shape.

• **Pacing is important.** Even the best-conditioned athlete cannot sprint at top speed for more than a couple hundred yards. In longer races, runners who start out at too quick a pace often find themselves lacking the strength needed to reach the finish line. In our lives, it is easy to fall into the speed trap, trying to live at a frenzied pace that is impossible to maintain for long. Hebrews 12:1 instructs us to "run with perseverance the race marked out for us," meaning we need to look beyond the crisis of the moment and live in such a way that we remain strong and effective throughout our lives.

Often, we accomplish more of significance in our lives if we resist the urge to rush faster and slow down instead. Proverbs 23:4 states, "Do not wear yourself out to get rich; have the wisdom to show restraint." Restraint is a practice that is simple to understand and helps us avoid many of the pitfalls of life, yet it is virtually nonexistent in our living-on-the-edge culture.

• **Pause to replace what the race takes out of you.** In a long-distance race, runners sweat out a lot of fluids. If those fluids aren't replaced throughout the race, the body will shut down as dehydration sets in. I once helped staff a water stop for a half-marathon race and was amazed at the number of runners who could not bring themselves to slow down long enough to successfully grab a cup of water. Too often I would see runners drop the cups or fumble with them as they went by, spilling most of the fluids their bodies would need to finish the race.

How often do we run by the water stops in our own lives? Do we continue to rush around day after day without pause until exhaustion or illness forces us to the sidelines? Do we experience sleepless nights in worry and anxiety while we rob ourselves of the rest we need to effectively tackle those situations? In Exodus 23:12, God commanded not only that the Israelites rest from their work, but also their animals and servants, so they would all be "refreshed." If we would like to be able to look back over our lives as Paul did in 2 Timothy 4:6-8, concluding that we have "fought the good fight" and "finished the race," we need to discipline ourselves to pause long enough to let God refresh us so we can finish the course He has mapped out for us.

Next Step

Take a few moments to reflect on your body in terms of rest. Can you say with enthusiasm that you approach each new week feeling genuinely refreshed? If not, commit to doing one of the following activities during the next week:

• If your nightly sleep averages less than eight hours, try going to bed a half hour earlier each night for the next week.

• Squeeze in time (preferably an hour or more) for simple relaxation. Some ideas may include sitting at a park or other natural setting, listening to relaxing music (not doing anything else but enjoying it), curling up in front of a crackling fire (not the TV) with the person or pet of your choice, or reclining in your tub or whirlpool.

• If you are an exercise junkie, take a day off from any sort of physical activity, perhaps substituting one of the "activities" from the preceding list.

• Try taking a nap in the afternoon, even if it is only for half an hour. The relaxation will do you good whether you actually doze off or not.

Notes:

1. Stephen R. Covey, A. Roger Merrill, and Rebecca R. Merrill, *First Things First* (New York: Simon & Schuster, 1994), p. 181.

2. Dr. Archibald D. Hart, *The Hidden Link Between Adrenalin and Stress* (Dallas: Word Publishing, 1991), p. 3.

3. Richard A. Swenson, M.D., *Margin* (Colorado Springs: NavPress, 1992), p. 122.

4. Hart, p. 21.

5. Hart, pp. 7, 31.

6. Diane Fassel, *Working Ourselves to Death* (San Francisco: HarperSanFrancisco: 1990), p. 44.

7. Hart, pp. 69-70.

8. Sleep survey data found in the press archives of the National Sleep Foundation Web site (http://www.sleepfoundation.org).

9. Stanley Coren, *Sleep Thieves: An Eye-opening Exploration into the Science and Mysteries of Sleep* (New York: The Free Press, 1996), pp. ix-x.

Chapter 4

A Mind at Rest

Joy looked up at the clock. It read 9:05 A.M., five minutes later than the last time she checked. In less than an hour she would know if she still had a job, but the wait was unbearable.

As Joy looked around at her coworkers, she could see the same worried expression she had noticed in the mirror all weekend. Naturally, the company waited until Friday to announce that it would be laying off workers on Monday so every employee could worry two extra days.

And worry was exactly what Joy did. All weekend she tried to figure out what might happen if her job was eliminated. Her husband, Bill, was already working for less money than he made a year ago, thanks to his company's last reorganization. In order to offset the loss of income, Joy recently accepted a promotion, even though it meant working longer hours. If she had stayed at her old job, she would be higher on the seniority list, meaning she wouldn't have to worry about a layoff.

Joy did nothing all weekend but let her thoughts torture her. When she tried to relax and think about something else, her mind raced through the list of bills that might not get paid without her paycheck. When she tried to sleep, she lay *awake stewing about the extra hours spent laboring over work projects to make sure they were perfect—time that now appeared to be wasted. When she tried to pray, her mind was distracted with worries about all that could go wrong if her job ended. She couldn't even remember the topic of yesterday's sermon.*

The ring of a phone startled Joy. When she realized it was not her phone, she was relieved. The call was for Anne, and Joy could tell from the expression on her face that she was being summoned into the manager's office. Every five or ten minutes, another phone in the area would ring and a fellow worker would walk off trembling to his or her termination.

Finally, the manager emerged from her office and announced that there would be a brief meeting in the conference room for the remaining employees. Joy's job was secure for now. As she walked down the hall, her emotions turned from worry into anger. She had just wasted an entire weekend worrying over a situation that never materialized.

Resting the body seems easy compared to slowing the mind. We can try to unwind or take a nap, yet our brains race to remind us of all that remains undone, unresolved, or uncertain. Real rest requires us to unplug our minds periodically from the countless to-do and to-worry lists we keep in our heads if not on paper. Those "lists" reflect two key aspects of our lives that can wear us down mentally when dwelled upon excessively: doing and worrying. Let's spend some time looking at each of them.

Addicted to Doing

In my first book, *Thank God It's Monday*, I devoted a chapter to helping readers avoid work addiction. After writing chapters touting the value of everyday work in God's eyes, I felt the need to include God's views on rest so that people didn't develop an unbalanced attitude toward work.

Since then, it has become clear to me that the problem most of us grapple with is broader than mere work addiction. Not all of us are addicted to work (although the numbers are large and growing). A far greater number of us could be considered "activity addicts"—that is, we are addicted to doing. We value doing something—anything—over "passive" things like pondering, praying, and resting.

I cannot count the number of people who have said to me that they cannot imagine ever just sitting around doing nothing. They say they need to be busy doing something productive or at least enjoyable. Idleness, even for the shortest of moments, is something to avoid at all costs.

Are you one of those people who can't stand doing nothing? Guess what? You just might be addicted to doing. Behavioral experts commonly cite the inability to relax or do nothing as a sign of activity-oriented addictions such as workaholism, compulsivity, and drivenness. Doctors Hemfelt, Minirth, and Meier contend that the drive to do can change one from a human being to a human doing:

> Humans *doing* ... are convinced they have to prove their worth every day. They feel that they must always be doing, accomplishing, performing, and perfecting in order to deserve their place in their family, their work, and their "system." Their motives are all wrong. They are driven by deep, underlying, unconscious motives, such as insecurity, fear, anger, and shame. Humans being might jot down fifty chores on their things-to-do list, accomplish only four, and still feel satisfied with themselves. Humans doing can complete all fifty tasks and then spend the rest of the day wringing their hands wondering whether they performed well enough, or whether they were too easy on themselves and should have tackled sixty or sixty-five jobs instead of fifty. [1]

Why can't we stop our endless cycle of activity? The emotions of insecurity, fear, anger, and shame just mentioned can certainly play a role for many people; but there are other reasons.

• **We adopt the world's perspective in place of God's eternal perspective.** Unlike most of us, God is not in a hurry. Throughout the Bible, He would take years, sometimes centuries, to accomplish His purpose. Jesus, despite having a ministry that lasted just three years, was never depicted as being in a rush. During His time on earth, there were so many people He never got to speak to or heal—yet the eternal impact of what He did goes beyond measurement.

When we lose sight of God's eternal perspective, we are influenced by the world's shortsighted, self-centered approach to life. People who believe life on this earth is all there is tend to want to cram that life with as many experiences as possible. This desire to experience everything leads to what some call "hurry sickness." Tim Hansel explains the allure of hurriedness:

> Our world seems intoxicated with hurry. It seems to be inundated with a hurricane desire to precipitate the future. One of the greatest sins of this age may be hurry. For in our impatient desire to make things happen, we have, inadvertently, overlooked what was really important. [2]

Here's a brief exercise to help you discover whether you might be suffering from hurry sickness. Sit quietly and try to estimate when a minute has passed, without counting or looking at a clock. You might have someone else time you or use a stopwatch (keep it out of view and stop it when you think one minute has passed). Many hurried people think a minute has gone by after only twenty seconds or so.

• **We attempt to do too much.** Frequently, people don't slow down because they are attempting to do more than they are capable of accomplishing. When we do that, we are always behind schedule, always playing catch-up. As we fall further behind, our tendency is to try to run faster instead of accepting the fact that we need to lighten our load.

In our culture, if we try to do everything those around us say we ought to do, we will inevitably become overloaded. *Self* magazine tallied up the time it would take for a person to follow the advice of "experts seeking to make us models of psychological and physical perfection." You can follow all these prescriptions for perfection, but only if you are somehow able to find thirty-five hours in the day. [3]

• **We are hooked on the adrenaline produced by hectic living and don't want to face the consequences of stopping.** As we saw in the last chapter, our minds and bodies can become dependent on the adrenaline produced during continued high-stress activities. Just as adrenaline can produce a "high" similar to certain drugs, ceasing activity can produce a crash much like drug withdrawal. The strong compulsion to do something and the feelings of guilt or depression if one stops are all considered signs of adrenaline withdrawal. [4]

• **We are afraid to stop because we might have to face up to what we have been avoiding.** Some people stay continuously busy because they are afraid to stop. Stopping gives us time to think, and thinking might bring forth all the fears and other issues we have avoided. If we are distracted from thinking, we don't have to deal with anything heavy. It is as if we believe that ignoring our problems will make them go away. Many people "keep busy" so they don't have to deal with issues such as a struggling marriage, the death of a loved one, life/career direction, sin, or their relationship with God.

I know of one woman who always kept busy and never spent more than a few minutes alone. She invited people over frequently and constantly volunteered to baby-sit for family and friends. It is normal to want to be with people, but it is not normal to be afraid to spend time alone. Often that fear is based on what we are afraid to think about when we run out of distractions.

• **We feel guilty about doing nothing.** Many feel that God is a stern taskmaster who will disapprove if we pause from our activities for more than a quick breather. We act as if we believe well-known but nonbiblical messages such as "idleness is the devil's workshop" and "God helps those who help themselves." It is as if we believe we can earn God's love and approval (and the approval of others) through working ourselves ragged. Yet, according to Doug Sherman and William Hendricks, God is not the One pleased with our heavy load:

If idle hands are the devil's workshop, then overly busy hands are his recreation. He loves to see people too busy to take time for God, too hurried to give any thought to the moral and ethical dimensions of what they're doing. [5]

"Better keep busy" and "better go faster" are common sentiments in our culture. How radically they differ from God's commands:

- Be still before the Lord and wait patiently for him (Psalm 37:7).
- Be still, and know that I am God (Psalm 46:10).
- The wisdom of the prudent is to give thought to their ways (Proverbs 14:8).
- It is not good to have zeal without knowledge, nor to be hasty and miss the way (Proverbs 19:2).
- For my yoke is easy and my burden is light (Matthew 11:30).
- The end of all things is near. Therefore be clear minded and self-controlled so that you can pray (1 Peter 4:7).

God is more concerned with who we are than what we do. Changing who we are involves time for thinking, reflection, and prayer. Paul writes in Romans 12:2 that we are no longer to conform to the pattern of this world, but "be transformed by the renewing of your mind." Real rest requires us to buck the world's busyness for awhile so we can renew and refresh our minds.

Much Ado about Nothing

Battling our to-do lists is a tangible problem. Worry, on the other hand, is an invisible foe. Instead of dealing with an actual situation, worry concerns itself with what *might* happen. Since none of us knows for sure what will happen tomorrow, our list of potential things to worry about is inexhaustible. We start by worrying about ourselves, then our family, then work, then our community, then our nation—it never stops.

Worry and anxiety are all-consuming emotions. It is difficult to be just a little worried or a tad anxious. The fear often takes control and affects everything we do or think about. It certainly makes meaningful rest difficult. You could spend all day lounging on the sofa and still not feel very rested if your mind is distracted with anxious thoughts.

Anxiety is a tricky emotion to escape because it operates independent of our actual circumstances. It can keep us from enjoying happy times because we are worried they will not last. Bad circumstances

48

become intolerable because we can imagine how things could get even worse.

Consider Job. Most of us are familiar with the story: God depicts Job as "blameless" and one who "shuns evil." Satan says that Job is good only because God has made his life good. So God allows Satan to take everything away from Job except his life. Although Job was bitter and angry, he did not abandon his faith in God.

Certainly Job did not appear to be at rest while he was going through his trials, but what about beforehand? he last time I read through the Book of Job I noticed a couple of verses that indicate that he might have been struggling with anxiety before he had anything to be anxious about: "What I feared has come upon me; what I dreaded has happened to me. I have no peace, no quietness; I have no rest, but only turmoil" (Job 3:25-26).

Despite having vast riches and a family to be proud of, Job "feared" and "dreaded" losing it all. Now fear and dread seem incompatible with the outwardly idyllic life Job lived before he was afflicted. Even though he had it all, worry appears to have kept Job from fully enjoying his prosperity.

Our culture is much like Job in this respect. The United States is by virtually every measure the most materially prosperous country that ever existed. I once heard that the average family in the United States is wealthier than 95 percent of the people who have ever lived on this earth. I wasn't able to see how that statistic was determined, but I think it puts our nation's wealth in proper perspective. We need to understand that when the Bible mentions the rich, it is not only referring to Bill Gates and other billionaires. It includes a lot of us who complain that our three-bedroom homes aren't roomy enough, or grumble about the payments on the two shiny vehicles sitting in our garages.

Despite—or more likely because of—our enormous wealth, we live in a society filled with worried, depressed people. If those visiting physician offices are typical, the current state of mental health is shaky at best, according to Dr. Richard Swenson:

Ask physicians about the frequency of anxiety or depression they find in their patients, and you will be stunned to learn how few in our midst are emotionally healthy and well rested. We worry about our jobs, our marriages, our children, our looks, our age, our health, and our future. The unacceptably high rate of tranquilizer use is a reliable indicator of our lack of emotional rest. [6]

Dr. Frank Minirth of the famed Minirth-Meier Clinic is known to frequently repeat the axiom, "Anxiety is a signal to relax and look for the source." [7] The situations that trigger worry vary from person to person, but I think the root of all our anxiety is the same. At its core, anxiety is a faith issue.

If we are to decide with whom to place our faith and trust, we have three choices: ourselves, others, or God. In our self-reliant culture, many of us trust no one but ourselves. We actually believe that we can control the circumstances around us to bring us happiness. Taking total control of our own life in this chaotic world is a huge responsibility. No wonder people are worried!

We can also become too dependent on other people for our happiness. This can lead to anxiety because those other people are imperfect like us. When the ones we trust stumble or our relationship with them is affected, our worries multiply. I once talked to a middle-aged woman whose husband had died a couple years earlier. It was clear to me that she had depended completely on her husband and was quite overwhelmed about what to do with her life. Once she discovered that God had a specific plan for her—not just through her husband—her anxieties began to fade away.

Joyce Meyer puts it well: "We should love people, but trust God." [8] God is the One who created and runs the universe, not us. When we worry about situations we can't control, we are in essence telling God we don't believe "in all things God works for the good of those who love him" (Romans 8:28). When we fret about upcoming decisions, we show our lack of trust, disregarding God's promise to "make [our] paths straight" when we trust Him with all our heart (Proverbs 3:5-6). If we are carrying a heavy load of worries in this life it is probably because we have a shortage of faith.

God clearly instructs us not to worry and provides a simple prescription for ridding ourselves of anxiety: "Do not be anxious about anything, but in everything, by prayer and petition, with thanksgiving, present your requests to God. And the peace of God, which transcends all understanding, will guard your hearts and your minds in Christ Jesus" (Philippians 4:6-7).

For me, this is the most powerful passage of Scripture in terms of finding rest for the mind. Instead of worrying about a situation, pray to God about it or as 1 Peter 5:7 states, "Cast all your anxiety on him because he cares for you."

When we faithfully bring our worries to God through prayer, we can experience an immediate and miraculous answer to our prayers. Will God take away the situation we are worrying about? Perhaps not. God does promise, however, to take the worry out of the situation. We bring God our anxieties and we receive in exchange His peace. Who could ask for a better deal than that?

Many Christians I know have experienced this immediate peace by casting their anxieties upon the Lord. Even so, I catch myself starting to worry sometimes. As I write this chapter I can see a mountain of work ahead of me on the calendar. In addition to researching and writing this book, I am teaching two new courses at a nearby college, developing and teaching a class on rest for community education programs, and guest preaching. While I prepare for my classes, I catch myself worrying about finding enough time to finish this book. When I write, I feel anxious about all the preparations necessary for my next class.

It has taken me a long time to realize that my only job is to work at the tasks God has given me to do today. Worrying about what needs to be done tomorrow—or what unforeseen event might happen tomorrow—is not my job. Jesus assures us in Matthew 6:25-34 that God will take good care of tomorrow for us:

Therefore I tell you, do not worry about your life, what you will eat or drink; or about your body, what you will wear. Is not life more important than food, and the body more important than clothes? Look at the birds of the air; they do not sow or reap or store away in barns, and yet your heavenly Father feeds them. Are you not much more valuable than they? Who of you by worrying can add a single hour to his life?

And why do you worry about clothes? See how the lilies of the field grow. They do not labor or spin. Yet I tell you that not even Solomon in all his splendor was dressed like one of these. If that is how God clothes the grass of the field, which is here today and tomorrow is thrown into the fire, will he not much more clothe you, O you of little faith? So do not worry, saying, "What shall we eat?" or "What shall we drink?" or "What shall we wear?" For the pagans run after all these things, and your heavenly Father knows that you need them. But seek first his kingdom and his righteousness, and all these things will be given to you as well. Therefore do not worry about tomorrow, for tomorrow will worry about itself. Each day has enough trouble of its own.

The last statement, "Each day has enough trouble of its own," is especially revealing. Jesus is aware of the struggles of everyday life—He experienced them Himself. He is telling us not to add anxiety about tomorrow to the challenges of today. To do so is to shoulder a heavy, exhausting burden—an unnecessary one given God's promise to care for those who seek Him.

Christ's message to us is that our primary task in life is to seek God. When we keep our focus on God and seek out His will and direction for our lives, we do not need to be anxious about the mundane things everyone else worries about. He promises to take care of those needs. If we truly believe in Him, we have no reason to worry.

The story of Mary and Martha (found in Luke 10:38-42) vividly illustrates the difference between God-seekers and worldly-worriers. The two sisters opened their home to Jesus and His disciples, but Mary spent her time listening at the feet of Jesus while Martha was distracted by all the preparations involved in having guests. Eventually, Martha grew upset that she was doing all the work and came to Jesus to fix the problem, saying, "Lord, don't you care that my sister has left me to do the work by myself? Tell her to help me!" (verse 40).

Jesus gave her an unexpected answer. "Martha, Martha. . . . You are worried and upset about many things, but only one thing is needed. Mary has chosen what is better, and it will not be taken away from her" (verses 41-42).

When I teach from this passage, I am struck by the number of people who admit that they can relate better to Martha than to Mary. Martha is a doer, while Mary just sits there. If Jesus suddenly showed up at our door someday, many of us would dive right in with our host or hostess duties, eager to do whatever we could to help. We would clean the guestroom as it had never been cleaned before and would attempt to cook for our Lord the best meal this side of heaven. Like Martha, we might find ourselves so caught up in our preparations that we would forget that Jesus was in our home sharing divine wisdom—and we were missing it!

The lesson Jesus teaches Martha—an accomplished doer and worrier—is critical to those of us seeking rest for our minds. He does not need us to do anything for Him or to worry about the status of God's plans. Instead of going off on our own doing whatever we feel is necessary, Jesus wants us to first come sit at His feet and listen. Every day we have the opportunity to sit with Jesus in our homes as we pray and read God's Word. We can lay our troubles and burdens at His feet and receive peace, rest, and guidance for the day ahead.

Stopping to rest with Jesus transforms our normal cycle of work, stress, and fatigue. Instead of wearing down by trying to do things for God, ourselves, and others, we are renewed as God works in His strength through us.

Next Step

Take some time to think about the things in life you tend to worry about. Then, complete the following sentence in the space provided:

My number-one worry is_____

_____

_____.

For the next week or more, take this worry to God each day in prayer. Turn over that worry to Him and ask for His peace about the situation. Pray for the faith you need to trust Him to provide what is best according to His will. If you start to feel anxious about the situation at any time during the week, stop immediately and begin praying.

Notes:

1. Dr. Robert Hemfelt, Dr. Frank Minirth, and Dr. Paul Meier, *We Are Driven* (Carmel, New York: Guideposts, 1991), p. 13.

2. Tim Hansel, *When I Relax I Feel Guilty* (Colorado Springs: Chariot Victor Publishing, 1979), p. 84-5.

3. "The 35-Hour Day," *Self*, April 1998, p. 169.

4. Dr. Archibald D. Hart, *The Hidden Link Between Adrenalin and Stress* (Dallas: Word Publishing, 1991), p. 71.

5. Doug Sherman and William Hendricks, *Keeping Your Ethical Edge Sharp* (Colorado Springs: NavPress, 1990), p. 195.

6. Richard A. Swenson, M.D., *Margin* (Colorado Springs: NavPress, 1992), p. 230.

7. Don Hawkins, *Overworked* (Chicago: Moody Press, 1996), p. 206.

8. Joyce Meyer, *Be Anxious for Nothing* (Tulsa: Harrison House, 1998), p. 75.

Chapter 5

A Heart Full of Contentment

Oh Lord, bless this quiet time when I come before you humbly in prayer."

Of course it won't be a quiet time next time we see Bob and Judy. The nerve of them, calling the police about Tuffy's barking. And to think of all the times we took in their mail while they were on vacation. How ungrateful can you get? You would think they might have had the decency to call us first.

"Uh, oops...sorry, Lord. Please forgive me for my sins and thank You for all that You have provided."

I'd be especially grateful if someone, who will remain nameless, could go just a single day without using all our credit cards, so we might have a fighting chance of paying off a few of our bills this month.

"Lord, not that I'm complaining, but if You could spare a few dollars to send our way, we'd greatly appreciate it. We might even be able to put more in the collection plate at church. Oh, yes, I lift up Your church throughout the world, especially our local church."

Why is it that Greg and Sue's children get picked for all the good parts in

the church dramas? Katy and Zach have just as much talent as those kids.
One of these days, some talent scout will be in the audience and it will be
their children who get the big break....

"...of course, Lord, it's not necessary that our children become rich and
famous celebrities. Okay, I must admit I'd rather be designing a brand new
beachfront mansion than repainting our boring old house...even though we
are thankful for that boring, er, nice house. I mean, we could have it worse,
given all the starving children in Africa and all that.

"Lord, I pray for all the lost, unsaved people of the world, especially my
boss."

What a jerk! Can't he see we're understaffed? "Why don't you all work a
little harder," he says. If he ever stayed around past 4:30 he would see that
none of us leaves for home much before 7. I told him that we couldn't possi-
bly meet our client's deadline if he decided not to replace Keith and Sarah
when they left. But did he listen to me? No! Whenever I tell him what we
need, he always rolls his eyes and smirks like he doesn't believe a word I say.
What if I suddenly stopped working late or—better yet—quit? Boy, then his
pretty little fantasy world would come crashing down around him.

"Oh...ah, well, in Your name I pray. Amen."

In a lot of ways, this chapter picks up where the last chapter left off,
since the two topics are closely related. Anxiety is worrying about what
you might be getting next. Lack of contentment is not wanting what
you have now.

When we lack contentment in certain aspects of our lives, rest is a
difficult thing to achieve. So is meaningful prayer time. Although I
hope my prayers don't sound quite as pathetic as the prayer just depicted, I sometimes find myself just as easily distracted. If you are like me,
staying focused during prayer right after a disagreement with another
person can seem futile. Other worldly thoughts can also disrupt prayer.
I frequently spend time with God during walks on the beach, yet several times I have caught myself trying to decide which beachfront home I
would like to own if I could afford one.

Rest for the body can be achieved by doing or not doing certain
things. Rest for the mind requires changes in our practices and thinking.

Rest for the heart, however, deals primarily with how a person feels about one's life. A person whose heart is dissatisfied with all or certain aspects of life will not find meaningful rest.

The Heart Deserves Special Attention

As a bodily organ, our heart is central to life. When it stops beating, life is over. Our emotional heart serves an equally important role, according to God's Word. The term *heart*, which appears nearly eight hundred times throughout the Bible, literally means "the inner man." [1] Proverbs 4:23 states, "Above all else, guard your heart, for it is the well-spring of life." Our hearts are the core of all we believe, feel, say, and do.

• Paul writes in Romans 10:9-10 that salvation comes from confessing with our mouths and believing in our hearts that Jesus is Lord, "for it is with your heart that you believe and are justified." Proverbs 3:5 instructs the reader to trust the Lord with "all your heart."
• The Valentine's Day tradition of handing out cards with hearts on them to people we care about is no accident. In 1 Peter 1:22 believers are encouraged to "love one another deeply, from the heart."
• The heart stores up whatever we feed our inner person—good or evil. Out of that storehouse flow our words and actions, according to Luke 6:45. "The good man brings good things out of the good stored up in his heart, and the evil man brings evil things out of the evil stored up in his heart. For out of the overflow of his heart his mouth speaks."

I think one of the most truthful depictions of the heart appears in Proverbs 27:19: "As water reflects a face, so a man's heart reflects the man." So many people in our culture are concerned about their image—what others think about them—but the heart reveals who they really are underneath the facade.

A Heavy Heart

We live in a world that lays a heavy burden on the heart. Think of the common expressions that point to pain in the heart. We can be weighed down by a heavy heart. Or experience heartache. Or have our hearts broken. Or have a heart that longs for something, be it another person, material wealth, or a better life situation.

Scripture talks about the heart using much the same language. The Book of Proverbs speaks to the anxious heart that "weighs a man down" (12:25), hope deferred that "makes the heart sick" (13:12), as well as the heartache that "crushes the spirit" (15:13).

Burdens and hurts that weigh heavily on the heart make us appear to be victims. Yet, at the core of a restless, heavy heart lie more evil intentions. Broken and hurting hearts are often filled with hatred, envy, various kinds of lusts, and selfish ambition. James 3:14-16 points out the source of these feelings, as well as the disorder and evil they create:

> But if you harbor bitter envy and selfish ambition in your hearts, do not boast about it or deny the truth. Such "wisdom" does not come down from heaven but is earthly, unspiritual, of the devil. For where you have envy and selfish ambition, there you find disorder and every evil practice.

Perhaps this sounds a bit extreme for your situation. Maybe the only issue you have is the desire for a little more paycheck each week. Or maybe it's a less stressful job or a more understanding spouse. How about a roomier house or a new car or an improvement in health?

None of those wishes sounds bad on the surface. Who doesn't want to improve his or her situation? Still, life dissatisfaction has a variety of sources, none of them particularly admirable. Four overlapping causes of discontentment are unfulfilled or unrealistic expectations, wanting what others have, ingratitude, and the desire for more.

Expectations Often Bring Disappointments

Sometimes our dissatisfaction is less determined by what happens than by what we think is going to happen. Expectations are a powerful influence in how we react to reality. When expectations are unrealistic, then we have problems. One our most unrealistic expectations is that happiness and contentment come from having the circumstances of life go the way we'd like them to go. We want career and financial success, a spouse who meets all our needs, children who grow up to make us proud, friends who look up to us—the list goes on.

Two problems are inherent with expecting that we will be happy when life goes our way. First, we are never able to fully arrange the circumstances of life to meet our ideal expectations. "In this world you will have trouble," Jesus said (John 16:33). The other problem is that even when we are able to meet our expectations in a certain circumstance, it doesn't make us deeply happy. We will likely agree with the writer of the Book of Ecclesiastes, who amassed all the wealth, pleasures, knowledge, achievements, and other positive worldly attributes, yet concluded, "Everything is meaningless."

As a child, I grew up with an extreme case of ambition. I remember, not long after learning to read, pointing to our encyclopedia set and telling my mother that someday I would be listed in that book. I wasn't sure if I would be so honored for my distinguished career in the U.S. Senate, starting up the next IBM, or for writing the book that defined the twentieth century. My expectations were geared toward achieving great things and being recognized for that greatness.

Most adults thought my childhood ambitions were cute or even admirable. Unfortunately, they took a lot of the fun out of growing up. I did not fully savor and cherish my achievements in school and beyond—as my mother did—because they were at best what I expected to happen. Besides, I "knew" that much better things were in store for me in the future. So I just took those achievements in stride. And failures—even small ones—were certain to rock the world of one who was supposed to be destined for greatness.

As my setbacks demonstrate, unfulfilled expectations can keep us from rest and lead us to despair. In addition, those unrealistic expectations can cause us to struggle incessantly to achieve the impossible. In fact, unrealistic expectations are a central characteristic of burnout victims, according to Dr. Herbert Freudenberger, one of the pioneers in the field. His definition of burnout: "To deplete oneself. To exhaust one's physical and mental resources. To wear oneself out by excessively striving to reach some unrealistic expectation imposed by oneself or by the values of society." [2]

The Grass Is Always Greener

The minute we start comparing our situation with others', we are in trouble. Having beautiful and talented children isn't enough. No, we have to enter them in pageants and other competitions to show that they are more beautiful and talented than other people's children. The satisfaction of a job well done used to be the reward most sought by workers. Now it's advancement up the organizational ladder with financial compensation to match. Each year I am amazed to hear of professional athletes with multimillion-dollar salaries who refuse to report to training camp because another millionaire of similar ability has signed a contract worth more money.

When we compare with others instead of valuing what we possess, we compete in a battle we can't win. We will always find someone better looking, richer, smarter, or more skilled than ourselves if we look hard enough. Comparing ourselves with others also robs us of rest, according to Tim Kimmel:

> The more we measure our significance by other people's accomplishments, the less we'll be able to feel at rest in our daily lives. A rushed lifestyle is only going to bring more successful people to envy, more unaffordable conveniences to covet, and more failures to regret. [3]

Proverbs 14:30 notes the toll such comparisons take: "A heart at peace gives life to the body, but envy rots the bones." Envy, which is to resent another for what he or she possesses, is closely related to the word *covet*, which means to intensely desire something, usually something belonging to someone else. *Coveting* is not a term used frequently today, but the Bible is mentions it a number of times. Whenever we strongly desire someone's situation or possession, we covet. And that, according to the tenth commandment, is sin: "You shall not covet your neighbor's house. You shall not covet your neighbor's wife, or his manservant or maidservant, his ox or donkey, or anything that belongs to your neighbor" (Exodus 20:17).

I must confess to having coveted houses. Right now, Kathy and I own a house perfectly adequate for all our needs: a 1960s split-entry home with three bedrooms upstairs plus a finished basement. It is an affordable home on a quiet street with great neighbors. Still, living in a coastal resort community, I have caught myself envying (and sometimes resenting) those people who can afford a second home much larger than my only home. In weak moments, I have also considered acquiring a nearby house with a panoramic ocean view should it ever be put up for sale. When I look around and compare, I begin to want what others have instead of being content with what God has already generously given me. Contentment is achieved only in the absence of envy.

Ungrateful in Paradise

When we have unrealistic expectations and constantly compare our situation with that of others, we tend to focus on our shortcomings instead of our blessings. Instead of praising God for His provisions, we tend to grumble about whatever is not quite right in our lives.

It is easy to feel angry and bitter about our negative circumstances, but most of us would do well to compare our situations with those who are experiencing real problems. As I work on this book, most countries in Asia are experiencing their worst economic crisis in decades. In Indonesia, 130 million of its 206 million people are living in poverty, compared to just 20 million two years earlier. Their government's version of a welfare program doesn't provide much of a safety net. Each family receives forty-four pounds of rice a month, plus health care.

If most of us were forced to eat nothing but rice, we'd probably grumble as the Israelites did in the desert when God provided them manna to eat every day. I doubt many of the Indonesians are complaining about the rice, given the alternative. The existence of ingratitude seems to run independent of one's actual circumstances, according to Henry David Thoreau:

However mean your life is, meet it and live it; do not shun it and call it hard names. It is not so bad as you are. It looks poorest when you are the richest. The fault-finder will find faults even in paradise. [4]

Do you think you would find faults in paradise? Ask those people who have won large lottery jackpots. Many of us would admit to feeling a touch of envy when we read of someone winning $50 million and living a life of luxury. It is interesting to note that studies of lottery winners indicate they are somewhat less happy than they were before winning their fortunes.

When we are ungrateful, we are essentially telling God that His blessings aren't good enough for us. We are saying that we don't believe the promise "in all things God works for the good of those who love him," found in Romans 8:28.

The Insatiable Desire for More

Underlying ingratitude, unrealistic expectations, and wanting what others have, lies the desire for more. When we are dissatisfied with our lives, trying to do more, be more, and get more naturally follows. This endless pursuit of more makes contentment impossible to achieve. Thus, it is no surprise that Dr. Freudenberger finds this drive to be a key characteristic of burnout victims:

> By setting themselves such high standards and pursuing them so fiercely, they insure their own discontent. Nothing is ever enough; every accomplishment leaves something to be desired. They rebuke themselves constantly for not doing more, being more, achieving more. They seem to have a constitutional inability to accept themselves for what they are, and a secret belief that other people wouldn't like them if they really knew them. Hence the image, the striving, the constant driving of themselves toward some elusive something. [5]

When we are dissatisfied with ourselves or some aspect of our lives, it is natural to try to fix the problem, fill the void. If we try to fill the void by improving our external circumstances with more money, things, or achievements, we will find that we constantly come up short. Take money, for instance. Ecclesiastes 5:10 states, "Whoever loves money never has money enough; whoever loves wealth is never satisfied with his income." Living in history's richest nation, one whose desired standard of living continues to escalate along with its debt, we see that verse in practice.

The desire for more certainly explains the pace of our culture. If you crave more money or achievements, you had better work harder. If you crave more life experiences, you need to pick up the pace. We have collectively moved the setting of society's daily living treadmill into high gear. Each year it becomes more difficult to avoid falling into step with those sprinting toward a finish line that always seems just barely out of reach.

God's Intent: A Content Heart

Life today can sound pretty meaningless. People rush about pursuing things that never quite satisfy, then they die. Is that all there is?

Fortunately, God cares about us much more than that. God wants to replace our restless, troubled heart with a heart filled with peace and contentment. Jesus said, "Do not let your hearts be troubled. Trust in God; trust also in me" (John 14:1). Paul said, "Let the peace of Christ rule in your hearts" (Colossians 3:15).

How do we end up with strong, peaceful hearts instead of restless, troubled ones? Contentment is the key. The world says you'll be happy when you have everything in life just the way you want it. God says you'll be happy when you learn to be content with whatever life brings—even if it is nothing like you thought you wanted.

In 1 Timothy 6:6, Paul noted that "godliness with contentment is great gain." Paul knew this from personal experience. His circumstances had ranged from being a well-off Roman citizen to being a prisoner in chains. God gave him the strength to find contentment in any situation:

I know what it is to be in need, and I know what it is to have plenty. I have learned the secret of being content in any and every situation, whether well fed or hungry, whether living in plenty or in want. I can do everything through him who gives me strength (Philippians 4:12-13).

Three lessons are clear from this passage. First, contentment is a learned behavior. As we have already noted, contentment does not come naturally for most people. It takes a concerted effort to rise above our circumstances and find peace. Second, contentment can be achieved in any situation, not just when things are going great. We do not need to obtain, attain, or achieve anything else to experience it. Finally, lasting contentment requires strength beyond our own, which of course only God can provide.

Learning contentment is, for most of us, a lifelong process. I can say with great confidence that I am considerably more content than I was ten years ago. I must also admit to frequent lapses in contentment, particularly during times of struggle. God is still teaching me volumes on the topic, even while I am working on this chapter.

How can we gauge our overall level of contentment? A simple method is to compare the time we spend appreciating our current situation with the time we spend wishing for something better. If phrases like "if only" or "as soon as" are a staple in your vocabulary, contentment probably doesn't describe your outlook. Don't worry; you are not alone. Most people could identify with at least one of these wish phrases: "if only I had a better job," "if only my spouse understood me better," "as soon as I make enough money," "as soon as our children leave home." Even one unfulfilled wish can rob us of contentment if we allow ourselves to dwell on it.

Cultivating Contentment

Although the practice of contentment is challenging in our culture, learning contentment is conceptually quite simple. Three keys to cultivating contentment are gratitude, acceptance, and service.

• **Gratitude.** The simplest and most effective means of gaining contentment is to develop the habit of being grateful. My favorite passage on being thankful is found in 1 Thessalonians 5:16-18: "Be joyful always; pray continually; give thanks in all circumstances, for this is God's will for you in Christ Jesus." Looking for God's will for your life? These verses contain a large part of His answer.

Every day of our lives should include a lengthy prayer of thanksgiving. According to St. Vincent DePaul, we should spend at least as much time thanking God for His blessings as we spend asking for them. At minimum, everyone should be able to thank God for giving us life, as well as sending His Son to earth to die for our sins. Giving thanks helps create contentment because it takes the focus off our problems and turns it toward God and His blessings. As we develop a spirit of gratitude, we can go throughout the day cherishing life's simple but wonderful pleasures, like the feel of warm sunshine on our faces or the smell of coffee brewing in the morning.

• **Acceptance.** Don Hawkins, in his book *Overworked*, wrote that "life is 10 percent what happens to me and 90 percent how I react to it!" [6] Difficult circumstances, personal shortcomings, and the imperfections of others lose their destructive power when we accept them. Acceptance does not mean we are to passively let life happen without lifting a finger to improve ourselves or our circumstances. That is called laziness. Acceptance involves liking who we are right now, even though we intend to grow over the years as we mature. Through Jesus Christ, God accepts us just as we are despite our sins, even though He promises to gradually transform us more and more into the image of His Son.

Acceptance also involves wanting what we have right now, even though we realize that circumstances will regularly change. It requires us to see God, not as a genie who grants all our wishes, but as a wise and loving Father who knows what we need infinitely better than we do. For example, small children can't understand why their parents make them work on chores and homework, instead of allowing them to spend all their time playing. Just as parents know that hard work builds character in a child, God knows that the struggles of everyday life build our character as well. Contentment requires us to trust God and live out the approach found in the serenity prayer penned by Reinhold Niebuhr: "O God, give us serenity to accept what cannot be changed, courage to change what should be changed, and wisdom to distinguish the one from the other." [7]

• **Service.** This third key to contentment is not as obvious as the first two, although I believe it is at least as important. When we serve God and others, it turns our attention away from our own problems and needs. When we help those in need, the reasons for our own discontentment seem petty by comparison.

Few acts are more selfless than serving others, yet when we complete our good deeds, we might experience even greater joy than those we have helped. As children of God, our ambitions should not lean toward fame and worldly wealth. Instead, the ambition of the contented is to be servants to others (Matthew 20:25-28), which allows us to follow Christ's command to store up treasures in heaven instead of on earth, "For where your treasure is, there your heart will be also" (Matthew 6:21). As we serve others, we store up heavenly treasures money can't buy, plus our hearts follow along to a far more restful place than the world can offer.

These steps to a contented heart are best pursued, not in isolation, but as part of a growing relationship with our Lord. Maxine Hancock, author of *Living on Less and Liking It More*, explains the connection well:

Contentment is the key to the restful, rejoicing Christian life. Godliness first. And then, with God at the center of our lives, contentment follows. Things become only as important as they should be: necessary to sustain physical life, but not necessary to build up our egos or to maintain a special status. As we mature in our walk with our Lord, things should lose their luster and their appeal. Certainly, the more time we spend looking into the face of Jesus in devotional worship, the less interest the things of this world will hold for us. [8]

Next Step
Spend at least an hour in quiet thought, reflecting on all the things for which you have to be thankful. Make a list of all the reasons that come to mind. Keep the list out where it can be seen every day, such as next

to your bed or desk (or even on the refrigerator). You may want to also use this list during your prayer time, especially when you are struggling with the desire for more.

Notes:

1. *The Zondervan Pictorial Encyclopedia of the Bible*, edited by Merrill C. Tenney (Grand Rapids, Michigan: Zondervan Publishing House, 1975), pp. 58-59.

2. Dr. Herbert J. Freudenberger, *Burn-Out: The High Cost of High Achievement* (New York: Anchor Press/Doubleday, 1980), p. 16.

3. Tim Kimmel, *Little House on the Freeway* (Portland, Oregon: Multnomah Press, 1987), p. 122.

4. Henry David Thoreau, *Walden and Other Writings* (New York: Bantam Books, 1962), p. 346.

5. Freudenberger, pp. 208-9.

6. Don Hawkins, *Overworked* (Chicago: Moody Press, 1996), p. 199.

7. Leith Anderson, *Making Happiness Happen* (Wheaton, Illinois: Victor Books, 1987), p. 21.

8. Maxine Hancock, *Living on Less and Liking It More* (Wheaton, Illinois: Victor Books, 1994), p. 139.

Chapter 6

A Soul Resting in Jesus

Jessie's ears perked up as she heard the familiar creak of the antique platform rocking chair in the study. Mr. Master must finally be settling down in a suitable chair to read. When he's working at his desk he never has room for a dog in his lap. Besides, chairs that roll on wheels don't stay in one place long enough for a napping dog.

After yawning and stretching her body, Jessie slowly padded down the hallway to the study. She so looked forward to being gently rocked to sleep in the warm lap of Mr. Master. It was the highlight of her day, next to barking at passing dogs and gnawing on her bone.

As she rounded the corner to enter the study, Jessie froze in her paw tracks. There was Johnny in her spot! Her mate of ten years had already made himself at home on the lap where she had planned to spend the next hour. Johnny preferred napping on Mrs. Master's lap, but since she wasn't home right now, he seemed content to take the next best spot available. He looked so peaceful, snoozing in comfort, so happy. Jessie was going to have to put an end to that. First, she scampered up to the edge of the chair and whined. No response. She rose up on her haunches, begging and waving her *front paws in an irresistible display of cuteness. Despite her efforts, no space opened up for her in the rocking chair.*

This situation called for desperate measures. With purpose, Jessie bounded into the living room to the window that looked out on the street. When she started barking at an apparent intruder, Johnny came roaring out of the study to join her. He fell for that ploy every time.

While Johnny searched in vain for a nonexistent intruder, Jessie slipped back into the study. The chair was empty. Her master had risen to scold the two barking dogs; now he returned to work at his desk. The day's opportunity for a lazy afternoon nap on a warm lap had passed.

Rest for the soul is hard to illustrate in worldly terms. Its closest comparison might be the peaceful expression on a small child's face as she's held by her mother. Another might be the security of a sheep in its shepherd's care or a dog on its master's lap.

Though not easily definable, rest for the soul may be the most important rest of all. For in the Bible, the word *soul* most commonly means life itself ("breath of life") or the inner life of a person. Soul might therefore be considered more encompassing than the body, mind, and heart. Because of that, rest for the soul does overlap with the other kinds of rest we have just examined. Still, it is given separate attention in the Bible, so I'll do the same in this book.

Soul is a frequently used term in God's Word; in my translation, it appears 139 times. The Bible repeatedly commands us to love and serve God with "all [our] heart and with all [our] soul." The soul or inner self is also where we bear the brunt of our trials and troubles. Looking only at the Book of Psalms, the soul is described as in anguish (Psalm 6:3; 31:7), filled with grief (31:9) and trouble (88:3), downcast (42:5-6; 43:5), forlorn (35:12), weary with sorrow (119:28), and refusing to be comforted (77:2).

The soul is most often referred to in relationship to God. The writers of the Psalms refer to the soul that pants (42:1) and thirsts for God (42:2; 63:1; 143:6), yearns for Him (84:2), longs for Him (119:20, 81), and waits for Him (130:5-6). Our soul is lifted up to the Lord (25:1, 86:4, 143:8), where it praises Him (103:1-2, 22; 104:1, 35; 146:1) and feels great joy (35:9; 94:19).

At the core of these Scripture verses is this truth: All of us have a longing deep within us to be united with our Creator. Why? One answer, based on biblical evidence and personal experience, is that God is the One who best meets the universal human needs for love and significance.

It is a rare individual who doesn't desire deep, genuine love. (This is not the same as the lustful romantic pursuit people call love, which may or may not last.) Yes, wouldn't it be great to be loved unconditionally, flaws and all? Wouldn't it be great to have someone who can see our true potential, instead of always noting when we come up short? Everyone craves the security of unconditional love, yet those who search for it in this world learn that it is scarcer than gold or diamonds.

Another universal yearning of the soul is the desire for significance. As a person reflects on his or her life, few things matter more than knowing that their existence has counted for something. It is natural for people to want to be important or be part of something important. How awful we would feel if our lives had no meaning: just grow up, go to school, work, get married, have kids, grow old and die. Does anyone start out intending to live a life that is meaningless and useless? Unfortunately, that is exactly how many people feel.

How does this relate to rest? Well, according to Dr. Herbert Freudenberger, to be engaged each day in activities that seem meaningless is an almost certain prescription for burnout. [1] When we lack love and purpose, we feel a void in our lives, an emptiness inside. That void gnaws at a person from the inside and prevents true rest.

Only once that we know of did Jesus express a sense of prolonged sorrow and unrest. In the last days of His life, Jesus knew the time had come for Him to die for the sins of the world. He who was without sin was willing to take all our sins to the cross with Him (see 2 Corinthians 5:21). In taking on our sins, He took on the punishment for those sins, which included death and a momentary separation from God the Father.

As He anticipated these events, Jesus experienced great anguish. "My soul is overwhelmed with sorrow to the point of death," Jesus prayed at Gethsemane the night He was arrested. I always thought the sorrow Jesus referred to related to His impending suffering and death.

Yet the explanation doesn't fit the situation. Was Jesus in sorrow over dying, even though He knew God would restore Him to life on the third day? Was the Son of God worried about the physical pain and humiliation of crucifixion? I don't think those things could bring the kind of extreme anguish in which His sweat flowed like drops of blood as He prayed.

What would create such trouble in the soul of Jesus? I think the only situation that could shake Him to the core would be His brief but total separation from God the Father. Since a perfect God can have nothing to do with sin, when Jesus took our sins to the cross with Him, He felt, for the only time in His existence, what life was like apart from God. No wonder He cried out on the cross, "My God, my God. Why have you abandoned me?"

The perfect union Jesus had had with the Father throughout eternity was severed, and it created anguish in the Son of God. Even though the separation was temporary, it appeared to bother Jesus more than being flogged and nailed to a cross in front of a jeering crowd. If being apart from God for a brief moment had such a troubling impact on Jesus, imagine the impact on those of us who are mere mortals struggling with living apart from God.

Unlike Jesus, most of us have felt the void of emptiness for more than just a few days. We have all had periods when we felt lonely and empty. Nearly all of us have experienced waves of pessimism, times when this life did not appear to have much worthwhile to offer. The fact that these feelings are common does not make them any less disturbing when we experience them.

Feeling the void in our lives is not the problem; it's what we do to try to fill the void. Many try to replace the emptiness with the best the world has to offer in the form of accomplishments, relationships, and riches. Surely once we are on top of the world we'll feel better, we tell ourselves. It becomes especially maddening then, when people wear themselves out trying to cram their lives full of these things, yet discover the emptiness inside still remains.

Many experts agree that the foundation of today's addictions, compulsions, and chronic busyness is our desire to fill the emptiness created by unmet spiritual needs. In their book *We Are Driven*, doctors of the

Minirth-Meier Clinic contend that the one driver behind every addiction and compulsion is "a quest for spirituality and more specifically a quest for God and the attributes of God." [2]

I was once taught that all people have within them a God-shaped void. What that means is that we were created to walk with God inside us, so when we try to live independently of Him, we feel the void of His absence. Despite filling our lives with good things, we eventually discover that nothing else can replace God. The writer of the Book of Ecclesiastes (thought to be King Solomon) sought out every pleasure and every worthy accomplishment and concluded that "everything was meaningless, a chasing after the wind; nothing was gained under the sun" (Ecclesiastes 2:11).

Those searching for spiritual rest—rest for the soul—will conclude as King David did in Psalm 62:1, "My soul finds rest in God alone." Although I will discuss how to find "soul rest" in greater detail in the next chapter, I want to spend a little time here looking at two visual images of a soul at rest found in the Bible.

Resting in the Care of the Shepherd

Psalm 23 is perhaps one of the most recognized portions of Scripture, often one of the first passages children are taught. It presents a peaceful, tranquil picture of sheep resting in the care of the Good Shepherd. Let's look at the first four verses:

> The Lord is my shepherd, I shall not be in want. He makes me lie down in green pastures, he leads me beside quiet waters, he restores my soul. He guides me in paths of righteousness for his name's sake. Even though I walk through the valley of the shadow of death, I will fear no evil, for you are with me; your rod and your staff, they comfort me.

Look at how completely God cares for us. He will give us more than just what we need; He will ensure that we will not be in want. This is not a guarantee of earthly riches, but an assurance of His provision for our best interest, including a secure place of rest. He will also restore our souls and guide us down the path of righteousness. Even in the most difficult times, He will be with us and comfort us. How could anyone feel restless in this Shepherd's care?

I had seen sheep before my trip to Ireland, but never so many of them. Woolly silhouettes dotted the entire landscape: mountains, valleys, cliffs, riverbanks, roadsides. None of the thousands of sheep in my view appeared to do anything more than eat and lie around in green grass, looking content with the world. Sometimes, when I'm in the middle of battling a deadline or a traffic jam, I must admit to being a little envious of critters that appear so carefree.

Why does the Bible speak of a relationship with God in these terms? The writer of this psalm was David, who grew up tending sheep and knew the value of a good shepherd. In my study of Psalm 23, I learned that sheep are neither the most intelligent of creatures, nor do they possess much in the way of natural defenses to protect themselves from attack. In fact, sheep can die by simply rolling over on their backs, since in certain situations they are unable to right themselves without assistance.

On their own or under poor care, sheep are fearful, restless creatures. Under a good shepherd—one who ensures they have access to adequate food, shelter, and protection—the same sheep can rest in quiet contentment. In fact, the mere sight of their trusted shepherd can quickly calm a frightened flock. The main difference between fearful sheep and contented sheep is the quality of the shepherd. The shepherd who cares for his or her sheep has their complete trust.

Psalm 23 is not the only reference to God as shepherd. Twice in John 10, Jesus proclaims, "I am the good shepherd. The good shepherd lays down his life for the sheep." We can have as our Shepherd One who knows our needs and has proved that He will go to the limit— demonstrated by His death on the cross—to enable us to have God in our hearts, filling the void of a restless soul.

Phillip Keller, author of A Shepherd Looks at Psalm 23, writes that having an all-knowing God as his Shepherd makes all the difference in his spiritual vitality:

If He is the Good Shepherd we can rest assured that He knows what

74

He is doing. This in and of itself should be sufficient to continually refresh and restore my soul. I know of nothing which so quiets and enlivens my own spiritual life as the knowledge that—"God knows what He is doing with me!" [3]

A Child with Its Mother

The second image of a soul at rest is also found in the Book of Psalms, Psalm 131:1-2:

My heart is not proud, O Lord, my eyes are not haughty; I do not concern myself with great matters or things too wonderful for me. But I have stilled and quieted my soul; like a weaned child with its mother, like a weaned child is my soul within me.

As a child, when I would fall and skin my knee, I remember how I would hobble home, bravely holding back the tears until I reached my mother. In her arms I no longer needed to be brave and strong. I felt safe enough to let all the tears flow. When she assured me that everything was going to be okay, I felt a sense of relief. Mom was going to make it better.

In a world filled with dysfunctional and disintegrating families, the peace a child experiences with his mother may be difficult for many to relate to without using considerable imagination. As adults, most of us realize we can never have that kind of comforting relationship with our earthly parents—even if we were fortunate enough to have it as a child. Now that we have grown up, we no longer see them as all-knowing parents who can make everything all right. At best, they become fellow adults with a little more experience and wisdom than we have. Often, as they grow older, parents begin to depend on their children for strength and help.

No, we can't go back to the security of our mother's arms for rest and comfort. We do, however, have the opportunity for that kind of peace and security on a more lasting basis with our Heavenly Father. Just as a child who has been weaned sees his mother as more than just a source of feeding, those of us maturing in our faith see God as more than just

Someone to answer our prayers when we are in trouble.

Jesus promises that in this world we will face troubles. When we shoulder the burdens of the world alone, we attempt to put on a brave front of pride to mask the fear, fatigue, and emptiness we feel inside. Only when we put aside our pride and accept God's love and guidance can we find a comfort far greater than the warm embrace of a mother—and a peace that we will never outgrow.

When we are at peace with God and walk with Him in our lives, we are less prone to the frantic pursuit of things this world finds important—things that will never fill the void in our soul. We also gain an inward rest that can prevail no matter what circumstances come our way. In the next chapter we will learn how to have that peaceful walk with God.

Next Step

Before moving on to the next section, take some time to evaluate how you currently stand in relationship to the four types of rest: rest for the body, mind, heart, and soul. For each category, give yourself a rating from 1 (miserable) to 10 (an example to all around you). In the areas with low ratings, jot down a couple reasons why you rate yourself so low. This information will help you better target what changes need to occur as you go through the remaining chapters.

Notes:

1. Dr. Herbert J. Freudenberger, *Burn-Out: The High Cost of High Achievement* (New York: Anchor Press/Doubleday, 1980), p. 165.
2. Dr. Robert Hemfelt, Dr. Frank Minirth, and Dr. Paul Meier, *We Are Driven* (Carmel, New York: Guideposts, 1991), p. 105.
3. Phillip Keller, *A Shepherd Looks at Psalm 23* (Grand Rapids, Michigan: Zondervan Publishing House, 1970), p. 69.

Part III:
Steps to Gaining Real Rest

After the first two sections of this book, you should have a better idea of how you measure up in terms of rest. Now what do we do about it? Is it God's will that we slog through the daily grind of life, wearing ourselves down until our bodies and minds give out? Does God want us to live life at a frantic pace, with schedules too jammed to pause to catch our breath?

Although Jesus never promises us a life free of troubles when we follow Him, He does offer far more than just the hope of a better life after this one is over. In John 10:10 Jesus says that He came that we "may have life, and have it to the full." He also prays in John 17:13 that His disciples "may have the full measure of my joy within them." Jesus not only promises us eternal life, but wants us to experience a full, joyful life here on earth.

The next six chapters cover some of God's provisions for a full, not frazzled, life. Some chapters deal with weighty topics like our relationship with Christ, while others deal with the more mundane details of how we schedule our time. When you are through with this section, you will have methods for gaining more rest on a daily, weekly, yearly, and even eternal basis.

Chapter 7

Enter God's Rest

D usk was fading away on this July Fourth evening. Soon fireworks would be thundering and cackling in the distance. I sat alone in my apartment, reflecting on my newly launched career and generally feeling sorry for myself.

I had started the summer with great ambition and hope. Just out of graduate school with an M.B.A. in marketing, I had big plans. First I would work on a contract basis for a local management consulting firm and then, within a couple years, implement my business plan to offer seminars and consulting services to nonprofit organizations.

Even by July I knew my plans were in trouble. My firm gave me only a fraction of the consulting hours I was anticipating, plus none of my efforts to bring in new business were panning out. In short, my efforts were failing, my bank balance was disappearing, and I was pretty much alone.

That night I sat in the dark and reflected on the first twenty-five years of my life. I remembered back to age thirteen when, at a baseball clinic, I prayed, inviting Jesus Christ into my heart to be my Lord and Savior. I started my walk with God with great fervor and determination. Over the years *something had gone wrong. I realized that I had gradually taken back control of my life from God. I was king of my castle once again, but the kingdom I ruled over was in ruins.*

On my own, I had made a mess of things. I had worn myself out worrying about situations I couldn't control instead of submitting to the One who had power over everything. In the midst of the explosion of distant fireworks, I looked up and said, "Lord, You've got all of me this time—and for good. Please change me."

From that day forward I have walked with the Lord and He has changed me for the better in more ways than I can count.

As we began to discover last chapter, the degree to which we experience rest in our lives depends greatly on whether we shoulder the burdens of the world ourselves or share them with the One who created the world. I know this to be true; I've tried it both ways.

Some of you may be tempted to skip over this chapter. Perhaps you've heard talk about having a personal relationship with Jesus Christ and don't want to hear it again. Perhaps you have already made such a commitment and don't think this chapter will speak to you.

I understand the tendency to want to skip over to more "practical" material. Please resist the urge. Unless you are already extremely well rested (and therefore reading this book for fun), you may find this the most important chapter in the book. If you are open to God's leading, working through this chapter could change your life. If you are already walking with God, you may discover how that relationship can help you gain more peace and rest in your daily life.

The Source of True and Lasting Rest

The Bible depicts God as the only source of true and lasting rest. The story of Israel's spiritual ups and downs is a perfect illustration of how our walk with God produces rest. When Israel's leaders and the bulk of her people followed God and His commands, Scripture repeatedly points out that God gave the Israelites rest, meaning the nation was at peace with its neighbors and at peace with itself.

Of course, those who have read the Old Testament know that the nation of Israel did not have a good track record for following God. The people and their leaders often forgot everything God had done for them and began to follow their own desires. Living apart from God, the Israelites had conflict with one another that split them into two kingdoms. When Israel faced another nation that threatened their peace, God fulfilled His promise to protect them as long as they relied on Him instead of their own military strength. However, despite dramatic instances of God single-handedly delivering huge armies into their hands, His chosen people more often than not chose to battle under their own power—and lost. Periodically, the Israelites would turn back to God, but usually only after their enemies had run them over and they realized how badly they had sinned.

Throughout history, God has promised rest and peace to those who follow Him—but there is no joy for those who go their own way. In the last chapter we looked at Psalm 62:1, which reads, "My soul finds rest in God alone." Consider two other Scriptures. In Jeremiah 6:16, the Old Testament prophet brought a message of rebuke to Israel:

This is what the Lord says: "Stand at the crossroads and look; ask for the ancient paths, ask where the good way is, and walk in it, and you will find rest for your souls. But you said, 'We will not walk in it.'"

Another Old Testament prophet, Isaiah, promises peace and healing to those who turn from their sins to follow Him. After this promise of hope to God's people Isaiah 57 concludes with the message, "But the wicked are like the tossing sea, which cannot rest, whose waves cast up mire and mud. 'There is no peace,' says my God, 'for the wicked'" (verses 20-21).

The Bible paints a vivid contrast between the restless sinner and the rested saint. Which waters would you rather experience in a small boat—the angry seas of the wicked or the "quiet waters" God promises us in Psalm 23? In my boating experience, I found nothing more restful than quietly gliding a boat through mirrorlike waters in the calm of the day, right around dawn or dusk. God promises to lead us to those quiet waters, even while we live in a world that often resembles a hurricane.

Jesus: Our Guide to God's Rest

Up to this point in the chapter, we have looked at examples and passages from the Old Testament. Eventually, God made it easier for us to enter into a relationship with Him and enter His rest: He sent His Son to show us the way. Jesus came to die for our sins and take them away, so we could regain fellowship with God. Jesus invites us to follow Him, to let Him be our guide. As we follow Him, He promises us the deep, inner rest of the soul we crave:

> Come to me, all you who are weary and burdened, and I will give you rest. Take my yoke upon you and learn from me, for I am gentle and humble in heart, and you will find rest for your souls. For my yoke is easy and my burden is light. (Matthew 11:28-30).

For all those worn out by the stresses and pressures of the world, Jesus offers an amazing promise. Enter into a relationship with Him, walk through your life with Him, and you will experience rest instead of weariness.

When I came to Jesus I was burdened with a faltering career and dwindling financial resources. I was on my own for the first time in my life and I didn't know if I was up to achieving what I had planned. Having Jesus in my life didn't bring about an immediate change in my outward circumstances. On the inside, however, knowing Him made all the difference, for I was no longer walking alone. I had Someone walking with me every step of the way, shouldering most of the weight of the world and guiding me in the path I should take. I found rest in Jesus.

Ten Rest Benefits of a Relationship with Jesus

How does knowing Jesus produce rest? The last passage we looked at only scratches the surface of God's provision of rest through His Son. In my search of Scripture, I have compiled a list of ten rest benefits of a relationship with Jesus that will help answer this question more fully.

1. Peace. *Peace* is a term that has meaning on several levels. At Christmas, many of us receive or send cards with the message, "Peace on Earth." Most people think of peace as the absence of armed conflict between nations. Individuals, too, experience peace when there is an absence of conflict within ourselves or between ourselves and God. To be at peace with a situation, for example, means that we have stopped struggling with it and started accepting it.

Jesus is referred to as the Prince of Peace in the Book of Isaiah, and throughout His ministry the words "go in peace" and "peace be with you" flowed frequently from His lips. Although the Bible contains many passages on peace, I want to concentrate on two from the Gospel of John, where Jesus gives final encouragement to His disciples before His death:

Peace I leave with you; my peace I give you. I do not give to you as the world gives. Do not let your hearts be troubled and do not be afraid. (John 14:27).

I have told you these things, so that in me you may have peace. In this world you will have trouble. But take heart! I have overcome the world. (John 16:33).

Several things impress me about these two passages. Most striking is the fact that the peace Christ gives us is His peace, the same peace He experiences with God the Father. In Him our sins are forgiven and our relationship with God becomes peaceful again. Nothing else the world offers can compare in value with this gift Christ gives freely.

In the second passage, Jesus promises His disciples that they will experience peace "in me." The peace Christ offers can be obtained only through our relationship with Him. Saint Augustine summarizes it well as he confesses to God, "Our hearts find no peace until they rest in you." [1]

2. Contentment. Since I spent much of chapter 5 discussing contentment, I won't dwell on it long here. Proverbs 19:23 states, "The fear of the Lord leads to life: Then one rests content, untouched by trouble." When we "fear" the Lord (which in this case means we recognize who God is and decide to trust, obey, and serve Him) and enter into a loving relationship with Him, what in the world could possibly trouble us? When we are loved and accepted by the One who created us, what worldly achievement could possibly be more fulfilling?

According to Henry Blackaby and Claude King, in their landmark book *Experiencing God*, our relationship with Christ provides the kind of contentment that takes away our compulsive need to do something in order to feel worthwhile:

> We are a "doing" people. We feel worthless or useless if we are not busy doing something. The Scripture leads us to understand that God is saying, "I want you to love Me above everything else. When you are in a relationship of love with Me, you have everything there is." To be loved by God is the highest relationship, the highest achievement, and the highest position in life. That does not mean you will never do anything as an expression of your love for Him. God will call you to obey Him and do whatever He asks of you. However, you do not need to be doing something to feel fulfilled. You are fulfilled completely in a relationship with God. When you are filled with Him, what else do you need? [2]

3. Quiet. We live in a hectic, noisy world. Quietness is becoming a more scarce and valuable commodity with each passing year. How many parents in households full of loud children say all they long for is a little peace and quiet?

In my own case, I can find true quietness only when I seek out God in prayer. When I slow down to be with God I find that, like the Psalmist David in Psalm 131, I have stilled and quieted my soul like a child with its mother. During my prayer time, I discover that God also leads me beside those same "quiet waters" David describes in Psalm 23. God provides quiet to His children out of love for us, according to Zephaniah 3:17: "The Lord your God is with you, he is mighty to save. He will take great delight in you, he will quiet you with his love, he will rejoice over you with singing."

Quiet is an important part of rest. In fact, in certain Bible passages like the one preceding, the word translated as "quiet" can also mean "rest." Being silent and being still are both part of being quiet—and part of resting. In my own case, I cannot have effective rest if it does not include some quiet times.

4. Light burdens. As we have already seen in Matthew 11:28-30, Jesus promises rest to the weary and burdened, assuring them that His yoke is easy and His burden is light. Why are the burdens of the world so much lighter when we have a relationship with Jesus? One answer is that we become yoked with Jesus. Although rarely seen in our culture, the yoke is a bar or wooden frame that is used to join two working animals (such as oxen) at the head or neck to maximize their pulling capacity. When we allow ourselves to be yoked together with Jesus, we have One who is immeasurably stronger than we are to bear the brunt of our burdens.

Another reason for our light burdens is that our relationship with Christ causes us to shed many of the loads we previously thought we had to carry. According to A.W. Tozer, in his book *The Pursuit of God*, some of the heaviest weights that drag us down are internal in nature, such as the burdens of pride, pretense, and artificiality. When we decide to live independently of God, that is the ultimate form of pride. To convince ourselves and others that we are up to the task, we tend to put our best foot forward—to look as if we have our act together. We anxiously hope that no one is able to look deep within us to discover our emptiness, our shortcomings, our weariness, and our desperation.

When we walk with Jesus, we don't need to appear like a god to ourselves or others. We don't have to be strong all the time because we can rely on the strength of the Son of God. We don't need to appear perfect, for Jesus accepts us sins and all. With those burdens lifted, we experience a rest Tozer describes as "the blessed relief which comes when we accept ourselves for what we are and cease to pretend." [3]

5. Assurance of eternal life. One of the great stresses common to all humans is the knowledge of our mortality. In our culture, people fight aging with all their might because they know that with aging inevitably comes death. Most of us don't think about death all the time, but the fear of it hangs over us, ready to grip us at the appropriate moment. To see the impact of that fear, pay attention to how people act at a funeral.

Or watch the facial expressions of a first-time visitor to a nursing home. The fear is real and can rob anyone of rest.

When we enter into a relationship with Jesus, death is no longer the dreaded end of life but the beginning of a wonderful eternal life with God. Because Jesus died for our sins, those of us who call Him our Lord will not face condemnation on Judgment Day. The Bible is clear that Jesus is the only means for obtaining eternal life:

> And this is the testimony: God has given us eternal life, and this life is in his Son. He who has the Son has life; he who does not have the Son of God does not have life. I write these things to you who believe in the name of the Son of God so that you may know that you have eternal life (1 John 5:11-13).

We do not merely have the possibility of eternal life; we can know that we have eternal life. Jesus is not our Savior only until the next time we mess up badly. When we give our heart to Him we can be assured that we are His forever. Jesus speaks of the certainty of salvation for His followers in John 10:28, "I give them eternal life, and they shall never perish; no one can snatch them out of my hand." For me, God's certain promise of eternal life takes away most of the dread of my eventual death here on earth.

Christ offers us more than just a more peaceful existence in this world. He offers a rest and peace that extends throughout eternity.

6. Hope that renews our strength. Hope is a simple but powerful emotion. The United States is a nation built on the hopes and dreams of its people. No other nation in history has been such a magnet for the hopeful, for the millions who traveled great distances to our shores in the simple hope for a better life.

When we hope for something, we desire it, plus we have some expectation that the desire will eventually be fulfilled. To not possess what we hope for is not a problem because we expect that situation to someday be corrected.

Loss of hope, on the other hand, is a crushing experience. The desire remains strong, but the person no longer expects to ever have the desire fulfilled. Many people experience a midlife crisis because they have reached a point in their lives when they believe that the great expectations of their youth will never be realized. Doctors at the Minirth-Meier Clinic say that loss of hope is one of the most common characteristics of the advanced burnout cases they see. Hundreds of their patients from all walks of life express the same emotion: "I just don't feel that there's any hope of changing the situation." [4]

People who possess hope have strength; people without hope are in many ways already dead inside. We need to understand that God is the ultimate power source and the best object of our hope. Nowhere in Scripture is the strengthening power of hope in God better expressed than in Isaiah 40:28-31:

> Do you not know? Have you not heard? The Lord is the everlasting God, the Creator of the ends of the earth. He will not grow tired or weary, and his understanding no one can fathom. He gives strength to the weary and increases the power of the weak. Even youths grow tired and weary, and young men stumble and fall; but those who hope in the Lord will renew their strength. They will soar on wings like eagles; they will run and not grow weary, they will walk and not be faint.

7. The perfect role model of endurance. In recent years it has become popular for Christians to display the initials to the question, "What would Jesus do?" The phrase was first made popular more than a century ago in the bestselling novel, *In His Steps*, written by Charles Sheldon. Christians in a local church turned a town upside-down for good when they committed to asking that question before they started any task.

Although I have yet to hear of a church successfully carrying out that commitment in real life (and, believe me, we would hear about it), Jesus did come to earth, in part, to make that kind of imitation possible. God did not send His only Son to earth merely as a sacrifice for our sins; Jesus was also a sinless man and thus, a perfect role model in how to live life right. The four New Testament gospels provide a substantial look at the life and teachings of Jesus so that, when He invites us to follow Him, we have a clear example to go by.

In Hebrews 12:2-3 we are asked to "fix our eyes on Jesus," to "consider him" who endured so much for our sins, "so that you will not grow weary and lose heart." When I catch myself getting worn down by life's trials, I find it helpful to reflect on the rejection and opposition Christ endured during His ministry on earth. My own pain and sorrows pale beside the excruciating experience of being nailed to a cross. If Jesus could endure all these things for me and others like me, certainly I can hold up under my own relatively minor inconveniences.

8. A cleansed conscience. Anyone who is a parent or has a parent knows the power of guilt. As a child I was one of the poorest liars around. The minute I would try to utter something other than the truth a sheepish look of guilt would spread over my face. I quickly learned it was easier to always tell the truth.

In a culture where relativism and diversity rule, sin is a term that has fallen out of favor. Even though we are not supposed to use such a label of shame to denounce our actions, the guilt produced by what we used to call sin still runs rampant. According to Ted Engstrom and David Juroe, guilt has had a devastating impact on the health and well-being of our culture:

> One must bear in mind that guilt conflicts can have a tremendously crippling, hampering, and tormenting effect upon one's life. In fact, this condition can lead to the outbreak of organic illness. Guilt is the key to compulsive behavior and is a major contributor toward a person's need to work excessively. Guilt can smolder within the recesses of the mind, causing innumerable problems. It can sour one's enjoyment of living, disillusion a person, and humiliate him. Along with hostility, it may be one of the two most significant variables in emotional illness. [5]

Although most of us view guilt in a negative light, it does serve a useful purpose. According to Tim Kimmel, guilt serves us spiritually in the same way a fever serves us physically. It tells us something has gone wrong that needs our attention. When we address the cause of the guilt instead of avoiding it, we can experience spiritual healing. [6]

Spiritual healing is central to Christ's mission here on earth. God created us to be His children, but since the Fall every one of us has been born into sin (Romans 3:23 says that "all have sinned"). Normally the penalty for our rebellion against God would be death and eternal separation from His presence, but God sent His Son to pay the penalty for all our sins and restore the broken relationship. [7]

When we have a relationship with Jesus Christ, guilt is no longer able to rob us of rest and peace. All our sins—past, present, and future—are forgiven. Guilt need not haunt us because Christ has been able, according to Hebrews 10:22, to "cleanse us from a guilty conscience." Freed from the burden of a lifetime of sins, we can face the future with renewed optimism and energy.

9. The power of the Holy Spirit. Most of us grew up learning at least a little about God and Jesus, His Son. We generally know considerably less about the Holy Spirit. Although this chapter emphasizes the role of Jesus in our rest, the Holy Spirit is also critically important. As Jesus was about to ascend into heaven, He promised His disciples and followers a special gift in Acts 1:8. "But you will receive power when the Holy Spirit comes on you; and you will be my witnesses in Jerusalem, and in all Judea and Samaria, and to the ends of the earth."

This Holy Spirit was initially received by a group of somewhat cowardly people, limited in their education and skill. Filled with the Spirit, these same people fearlessly proclaimed the Good News of Jesus Christ and founded a church that spread like wildfire. Many displayed wisdom that confounded the scholars of the day, while others were given healing powers more remarkable than modern medicine. Although the power of the Holy Spirit has been expressed in many different ways throughout the history of the church, one can clearly see that God regularly performs extraordinary works through ordinary people who are devoted to Him. Second Timothy 1:7 states that "God did not give us a spirit of timidity, but a spirit of power, of love and of self-discipline."

Do not underestimate the Holy Spirit's power. I first experienced the Spirit working through me when I was asked to teach adult Sunday School to a large congregation of singles. I was still a very young Christian with limited Bible knowledge. It did not help to know I would be teaching a class loaded with Christian college graduates and a number of seminary students.

With little knowledge or teaching experience to draw upon, I had to lean completely on God. As I researched and prepared for many hours, I was amazed at the insights that could have come only from the Holy Spirit. Before the class began, I committed the time to God, asking that the lesson not be taught by me but by Him through me. He answered that prayer in a big way as I felt the Holy Spirit teaching with God's power through me.

10. The fruit of the Spirit. When we accept Christ into our hearts and walk with Him, we receive more than just the power of His Spirit. Over time, God replaces the habits of our sinful nature with what Scripture calls "the fruit of the Spirit." Galatians 5:16-26 explains these contrasting natures. The sinful nature includes rest-robbing actions such as hatred, discord, jealousy, fits of rage, selfish ambition, and envy. As the Holy Spirit dwells within us, He begins to replace the sinful nature with His own fruit, which includes "love, joy, peace, patience, kindness, goodness, faithfulness, gentleness and self-control."

Most of us would admit to desiring more of this kind of fruit. It doesn't require great imagination to see how these traits could help create a life with less weariness and more rest. On our own power, however, our daily lives always seem to contain more of the petty anger and pride of our sinful nature than we would like to see. We gain the upper hand in improving our behavior when we allow God to focus on the heart of the matter—our hearts. When we make a commitment to follow Jesus and invite His Spirit to dwell in our hearts, God can transform us from the inside out into the person we always hoped we could be.

Next Step

The next step in applying this chapter is to spend some time evaluating your relationship with Jesus. Some of you may have made a commitment to Jesus before, but are not experiencing all of the rest benefits cited in this chapter. I would suggest spending at least an hour or two reflecting on your relationship with Jesus. If you are like me, it is easy to get so busy that you ignore God and gradually take back control of your life from Him. If that is your situation, you may want to pray to recommit your life to Christ and pray the upcoming prayer once again.

If you have not made such a commitment before, I urge you to review the material in the last couple of chapters, especially the Bible verses. Some additional verses you might want to look up in the New Testament include John 3:16; Romans 5:8, 6:23, 10:9, 10:13; Ephesians 2:8-9; 1 John 5:11-13; and Revelation 3:20. If you are tired of going it alone in life, the steps to receiving Christ are simple:

Admit that trying to live your life apart from God has been a mistake.

Be willing to turn your back on past mistakes and sins—and let Jesus guide you in the right way to live.

Believe in the promise of salvation: that Jesus Christ died for you on the cross and rose from the dead so that you might have eternal life.

Pray to invite Jesus Christ to come in and control your life through the Holy Spirit, thus receiving Him as your Lord and Savior. A sample prayer might go like this:

Jesus, I've tried to live my life on my own apart from You, and I haven't done a very good job of it. Please forgive me for all my sins—I want to turn away from them and leave them behind for good. I believe You died for my sins, rose from the dead, and stand ready to enter my heart to walk with me. Please come into my heart and save me. I want to follow You and make You Lord of my life. Thank You for hearing my prayer. Amen.

If you are not sure whether you want to make such a commitment, I recommend two organizations, the Luis Palau Evangelistic Association and the Billy Graham Evangelistic Association, that you may contact for more information and assistance (see footnote 8 for contact information).

For those of you who have decided to turn your life over to Christ, I would like to send or e-mail you a special short report, "Growing in Jesus," as a free gift. This report outlines a few simple steps that will help you grow in your relationship with Jesus Christ. When you write, I would appreciate hearing a word or two of the circumstances of your coming to Christ. You can find my business and e-mail address at the end of this book. Don't worry about your name ending up on some junk mail list. I won't even put you on my own mailing list unless you ask me to do so!

Notes:

1. Saint Augustine, *Confessions* (New York: Penguin Books, 1961), p. 21.
2. Henry T. Blackaby and Claude V. King, *Experiencing God* (Nashville: Broadman & Holman Publishers, 1994), p. 53.
3. A.W. Tozer, *The Pursuit of God* (Harrisburg, Pennsylvania: Christian Publications, Inc., 1948), p. 116.
4. Frank Minirth, Paul Meier, Don Hawkins, Chris Thurman, and Richard Flournoy, *Beating Burnout* (New York: Inspirational Press, 1997), p. 135.
5. Ted W. Engstrom and David J. Juroe, *The Work Trap* (Old Tappan, New Jersey: Fleming H. Revell, 1979, p. 144.
6. Tim Kimmel, *Little House on the Freeway* (Portland, Oregon: Multnomah Press, 1987), p. 75.
7. Here are some verses regarding the forgiveness of our sins that you may want to look up in your Bible: Romans 3:10-11, 5:12, Colossians 1:13-14, 2:13-14, 1 Peter 2:24, 3:18, 1 John 1:7-10.
8. If you have questions or would like more information about having a relationship with Jesus Christ, here are two organizations I have worked with that have resources available to help you in this decision:
• Luis Palau Evangelistic Association, P.O. Box 1173, Portland, OR 97207-1173, Phone: (503) 614-1500, e-mail: lpea@palau.org, Web site: www.gospelcom.net/lpea/.
• Billy Graham Evangelistic Association, P.O. 779, Minneapolis, MN 55440-0779, Phone: (887) 247-2426, e-mail: info@bgea.org, Web site: www.billygraham.org.

Chapter 8

Schedule Your Life with Purpose

M ary stirred the cream and sugar into her coffee as she thought of possible answers to Jenny's question. "What one additional thing could I do that would make the greatest difference in my personal or professional life?" Mary repeated the question out loud, hoping it would buy her some time.

"Not a question you think about every day, is it?" Jenny asked. "It took me quite a while to decide what I would do."

"And that would be?"

"Oh no you don't. You need to answer the question for yourself first."

It had been years since Mary had even thought about adding something new to her schedule. Most of the time she tried to figure out tasks and commitments she could drop or defer. It was tough to shift gears like this.

"I don't know if this answers your question, but I always regret not finishing my degree. It was something I willingly gave up to meet family obligations, but now with the children in school, I see how that degree would allow me to do more interesting and challenging work."

"Great, why don't you go ahead and do that?"

Mary shook her head at Jenny's youthful enthusiasm. "Sure, no problem. After taking care of my job, the kids, and the house, I think I'll add a few classes. Why didn't I think of that before?"

Jenny looked a little hurt. "I didn't mean to make you mad."

"No, I'm sorry. I didn't realize how much resentment I was feeling about not finishing school. By the way, how did you answer the question?"

Jenny's smile returned to her face. "One of my favorite activities has always been painting. It's exciting to create something new and at the same time it is so relaxing. I don't think I've picked up a brush in six months, though. This summer I've decided to rent a cabin in the mountains and do nothing but paint for a whole week. Maybe in the fall I'll open up a little studio out of our garage and teach children how to create and appreciate art. Doesn't that sound fun?"

Even though Mary was more of a paint-by-number type, she liked the idea. "Hey, I thought you were only supposed to come up with one thing? You picked two."

"Well . . . ah, I'll just do one . . . at a time."

A few of you might be wondering what a chapter on scheduling is doing in a book on rest. Shouldn't we be burning our schedules and calendars instead of learning new ways of using them better?

Actually, my decision to include this chapter comes from my desire to avoid subjecting readers to the same frustration I experienced while researching this topic. I read a lot of material on stress, burnout, and leading a simpler life. In many of the books—especially those taking a nonspiritual approach—the recommendations came in the form of fast and furious lists of items the reader needed to do right away. To me, giving a weary person a long to-do list is like handing a drowning person a bucket of water.

In this book, I will try to keep from adding too many items to your to-do list. Before I address further recommendations to help you find more rest, I want to cover some scheduling basics that will allow you to more easily create room in your schedule for whatever new "activities" you might decide to add.

Why the Rush?

It doesn't take much insight to notice that much of the world has increased its pace of living from a walk to an all-out sprint. For the most part, people are cramming more activity into each day than ever before, yet there is a growing sense that many important areas of life are left untouched and ignored. Sleep? Only when necessary. Exercise? Well, maybe next week. Prayer? Does saying "Lord, help me get through the day" while driving to work or school count? Family? As long as the five minutes we spend together at the breakfast table is called "quality" time, that's all that matters. Close friendships? Do childhood friends seen once a year count? Day of rest? Pipe dream.

Why the big hurry? Most people know only that they have a lot to do—and they're behind schedule. Personally, I think the replacement of religion as the centerpiece of society has contributed to the rush far more than any of us realize. In a secular culture, people don't think of eternity, just the here and now. If this life is all there is, then why bother to develop character and nurture relationships? Without an eternal perspective, people just stuff their lives full of as many experiences and activities as possible. Gains in technology have simply enabled many to raise their speed of hyperactivity to astounding levels.

As Christians, we who understand eternity should be a counterbalance to this cultural stampede. Unfortunately, we are too often running at the head of the pack. I've met many frantic, stressed-out people over the years and a disturbing percentage of them are Christians. Why? Many of us are trying to do everything the world demands of us, plus what we think God would want us to do. Of course we don't know what God would have us do because we don't stop long enough to ask—and wait for His response.

Tyranny of the Urgent

You and I can easily list the reasons for our busyness. I've found it more difficult to understand how people today do so much more, yet appear less able to manage their bodies, their relationships, and their spiritual lives. The best explanation I've found comes in a little pamphlet called "Tyranny of the Urgent," first published back in 1967. Charles Hummel asserts that people ignore what is most important in their lives because they have become slaves to the urgent:

> We live in constant tension between the urgent and the important. The problem is that many important tasks need not be done today, or even this week. Additional hours for prayer and Bible study, a visit to an elderly friend, reading an important book: these activities can usually wait a while longer. But often urgent, though less important, tasks call for immediate response and gobble up our time. Endless demands pressure every waking hour. . . .Their appeal seems irresistible, and they devour our energy. But in the light of eternity their momentary prominence fades. With a sense of loss we recall the important tasks that have been shunted aside. We realize that we have become slaves to the tyranny of the urgent. [1]

Our lives seem to have limitless options in terms of how to spend our time. With so many potential things to do, it is often the task that cries out loudest that gets our attention. I've had jobs where everything I worked on was considered "urgent" by those I worked for. I simply lined up the projects in terms of when they were due and, as long as I met my deadlines, everyone was happy—except me. I knew lots of ways I could help the company in more substantial ways, but there was never any time left after handling all those urgent requests.

Stephen Covey, in his best-selling books, *7 Habits of Highly Effective People* and *First Things First*, illustrates the tradeoff between the important and the urgent by creating a matrix with four quadrants. In the first quadrant are things that are both important and urgent, like crises, important meetings, and tight deadlines. These important tasks find their way onto our schedules because they are urgent. Covey labels the second quadrant the "Quadrant of Quality" because it contains important tasks that are not urgent like planning, relationship building, preparation, and recreation. These tasks are at least as important as Quadrant One activities but, because they aren't urgent, people keep putting them off and rarely get around to doing them. [2]

The third quadrant contains tasks that are unimportant but urgent. Examples include many of the interruptions, phone calls, routine

reports, and meetings that make up many of our days. The last quadrant, the unimportant and not urgent, include time wasters like junk
mail, television, and busywork. The key to effective living, according to
Covey, is to spend more time in Quadrant Two (important, not urgent)
activities and less time in Quadrants Three and Four. In a study con-
ducted by his firm, Covey found that executives of high-performance
organizations spent the majority of their time in Quadrant Two, while
executives in typical companies spent most of their time operating in
Quadrant Three. [3]

This "tyranny of the urgent" also explains why people who lug
around those huge daily planner notebooks are not always the most
organized and effective. Most people use time management tools to
merely prioritize and schedule the urgent, leaving many important areas
of life untouched because they didn't make it onto the list. As Charles
Hummel puts it, "The key is not to prioritize the activities on your
schedule, but to schedule your predetermined priorities." [4]

What's Important to God?

If we decide to orient our schedules toward what is important, it begs
the question, "What is important?" Ask ten people that question and
you may end up with ten different answers. Since God will be the ultimate Judge of what is important, let's see what His Word, the Bible,
deems critical for us to do.

First of all, the Bible is very clear that activities God values will be
different from what our culture values. Romans 12:2 states, "Do not
conform any longer to the pattern of this world, but be transformed by
the renewing of your mind. Then you will be able to test and approve
what God's will is—his good, pleasing and perfect will."

Those who attempt to do what both God and the world values will
find themselves facing an impossible task. The world urges us to hop on
a speeding treadmill of endless activity. God tells us to be still. The
world says that to find significance we must do something to achieve
fame or fortune. God is less concerned with what we do than in who
we are and—most importantly—who we are becoming as we walk with
Him. In scheduling your life, don't fool yourself by thinking that fol-

lowing God won't require a departure from the path most others travel. It will.

So what does God value more than the things most of the world values? I think much of what God deems important can be found by examining His two instructions of greatness: the Great Commandment and the Great Commission.

The Great Commandment is the response Jesus gave when asked which of God's commands is most important. Jesus answered (in Mark 12:30-31) that the most important command is, "Love the Lord your God with all your heart and with all your soul and with all your mind and with all your strength." The second most important is to love your neighbor as yourself.

What does God value? He wants us to love Him, ourselves (if we don't love ourselves, then loving our neighbor as ourselves has little value), and others with all that we are. That means loving relationships are His priority for us. As a task-oriented person who enjoys working alone, I previously found people to be a bit of an irritating interruption. Relationships didn't make my lengthy to-do list, which meant they only got in the way of my productivity. Over the years, God has taught me that most of the projects I thought were important had little lasting value. The relationships I build, on the other hand, can have eternal significance and consequences because those who become God's children will spend eternity together with Him.

The other great command of God is the Great Commission, found in Matthew 28:18-20. In the final verses of this gospel, the resurrected Jesus gives His followers their marching orders, telling them, "Go and make disciples of all nations, baptizing them in the name of the Father and of the Son and of the Holy Spirit, and teaching them to obey everything I have commanded you. And surely I am with you always, to the very end of the age."

Many people have reduced Christianity to merely attending church and trying to avoid sin. As we can see from these great commands, churchgoing and sin-avoiding are not the essence of Christ's teachings. The Great Commandment instructs us to love God and others, while the Great Commission tells us to "go and make disciples." Disciple-making can include a lot of things, but its focus is to help people find

Jesus and grow in their faith. This task, too, centers on relationships.

These great commands sound a little overwhelming at first, but God has provided more detailed instructions in His Word, plus a great role model in His Son. Ephesians 5:15-17 offers helpful wisdom as to how we are to live our lives. "Be very careful, then, how you live—not as unwise but as wise, making the most of every opportunity, because the days are evil. Therefore do not be foolish, but understand what the Lord's will is."

I see three important guidelines present in this passage. First, we need to approach our lives with care and wisdom, instead of just floating through our days without a thought or clue. Next, we need to be prepared to take advantage of the opportunities God places before us, meaning we should be ready to alter our ways as circumstances change. Finally, and most importantly, we need to have a sense of the will of God to help us find direction. As our relationship with God grows by spending time with Him in prayer and in His Word, He will begin to show us where He is working around us and how He wants to use us in that work.

We are not meant to operate independent of God the Father. Even Jesus said that He could do nothing apart from His Father. In John 14:31, Jesus tells His disciples, "I do exactly what my Father has commanded me." In a prayer to God in John 17:4, Jesus says, "I have brought you glory on earth by completing the work you gave me to do." Jesus understood His purpose and simply did what God asked Him to do each and every day of His life.

At the end of His life on earth, Jesus was able to say He completed all the work God had given Him. In God's eyes, Christ's life was a success. But with human eyes, the life of Jesus at the point of His crucifixion hardly appeared successful. A man with no wealth and no job had led a ragged group of followers who promptly fled at the first sign of trouble. His term of ministry was a scant three years and He barely put a dent in the ranks of the sick and hurting in Israel. He spent much of His time preparing twelve disciples for ministry, yet it was one of those leaders-in-training who had Jesus arrested. Those in the world without God's perspective couldn't possibly imagine the victory Jesus had won that day.

When we walk with Jesus, we too can play a role in that great victory. We can be part of a success the world can never understand. We can also be liberated from the oppressive, never-ending demands of the world's standards of success. Unlike worldly sources of work, God's work assignments come with both the time and the resources necessary to accomplish them.

Steps to Scheduling Your Life with Purpose

I have examined more schedule planners and books on scheduling than I would care to admit. There are hundreds of different planning systems on the market—and with good reason. We all plan our lives differently. Among the people I know, I've seen planning systems ranging from notes on paper napkins to notebooks larger than most briefcases.

My own scheduling system is part original, part adapted from other sources. It works fairly well for me, but I won't try to subject you to it. Instead, I will propose five steps to help you better schedule your life with purpose, regardless of the scheduling system you do or do not use.

Step 1: Identify the key roles and/or relationships in your life. In order to take a more biblical approach to scheduling, I have found it helpful to look at the key roles that I play in life and the key relationships within those roles. If our Great Commandment is to love God and "our neighbors," identifying those key neighbors is necessary before we get into any heavy life planning. In my own case, I find it helpful to categorize those relationships by the roles I play in interacting with them. For example, rather than listing all the types of students I teach, I combine those relationships under my role as teacher.

Six days a week I operate from a to-do list. I used to have a single weekly list, but I found more balance when I broke down my to-do lists by my roles in life. Currently the roles include child of God, self-care manager, husband/friend/family member, writer, entrepreneur, teacher, and career/financial manager. Most of my key nonwork relationships fall into those first three roles. I include myself under the people I am to care for, since the commandment says we are to love our neighbor "as yourself."

Step 2: Within each role or key relationship, identify one or two important areas you feel you have been neglecting. This might include a troubled friend you have been unable to visit. It might include improving your relationship with God by better developing the habit of regular prayer. The list you will develop will likely cover the important but not urgent areas of your life. I call this list of things I want to make more time for my "Important Want-to-Do" list. Don't forget your relationship with yourself either. This would be an appropriate place to list a personal development goal such as exercising or scheduling a Sabbath day of rest.

Do not neglect this step. The list you create could contain many of the important things you always wanted to do with your life. As we begin doing those things, we create a life lived with fewer regrets, because we didn't neglect important relationships or roles. According to Ted Engstrom and David Juroe, "One who can't decide what the important things in life are lets his life slip through his hands in little pieces." [5]

Step 3: Create a list of "less important now-do" activities. Adding new activities or habits to your schedule is easy as long as you have lots of "free" time available on your calendar. If you are like me, this is not the case. In order to create room for "important want-to-do" items, something has to be dropped from your schedule. This is where the "less important now-do" list comes in. These are activities you currently perform that you feel might be of less importance than the items on your first list. These may not be bad activities, but you may decide they are worth giving up to make room for something better.

Some of us can quickly identify our time-wasters. Others may need to conduct a comprehensive time log or inventory for a week to see where their time is going. Everyone should do such an inventory at least once in his or her life. When I did mine, I simply broke the entire week down into fifteen-minute segments and wrote down what I did during each segment. I discovered the things that I said were important to me represented a smaller proportion of my time than I thought they would. For example, I was surprised how much time I spent in front of the television compared to pursuits I said were of greater importance, like book reading and prayer. Based on that information, I set limits on the amount of television I watch each week (When you consider that the television is on in a typical U.S. household for nearly a forty-hour shift each week, setting this goal has redeemed a lot of hours for me).

If you dismiss doing a time log because you don't have time or don't think you can jot down all you do in a week, take warning. Experts say people with this attitude have already diagnosed themselves as driven individuals who are likely to have some sort of compulsive behavior problem or addiction. [6]

However you come up with your less important now-do list, you now have two lists that contain information to help you orient your life toward more important matters. Your less important list may contain some activities you enjoy, but if you compare them with your want-to-do list, you can see how your sacrifice will be small compared with the rewards of living a more balanced life.

Step 4: Pick one item from your important want-to-do list to work on during the next month. I find it difficult to change more than one habit at a time, so I recommend taking at least a month to work on just one activity from your want-to-do list. Perhaps you want to spend more time with your spouse or create time for a day of rest. If you are struggling to select an item, you may want to consider pondering the question the two women considered at the beginning of the chapter: What one additional thing could I do that would make the greatest difference in my personal or professional life? [7] Pick one item to work on, then turn to your less important now-do list and select a couple activities to phase out. I recommend selecting two activities to eliminate for every new addition, so that your schedule doesn't become any more jam-packed than it is already. If possible, do your added activity in the same time slot as the ones you are giving up. Try this for at least a month and, if you are successful, consider adding on another want-to-do activity.

When we moved to New England in 1996, I wanted to significantly increase my time in prayer. I created more room in my schedule by reducing two activities: commuting to work and reading the newspaper. With the move I automatically reduced my commute time since I now work out of the home more often, plus the college where I teach most often is just two miles away.

Up until the move, I had always subscribed to a daily newspaper. Although it kept me current with the news, I found that a large portion of my reading time was devoted to the sports section. I enjoyed pouring over the box scores from the important games played the night before. I had such a good eye for statistics that I could recite current batting averages for many of the players of my favorite baseball team.

Now much of the time I used to spend with the paper or in the car is spent with God. I've found it far more rewarding to increase my knowledge of the Bible than to know baseball batting averages.

Step 5: Be willing to let God mess up your schedule for His plans. One of the common frustrations with scheduling is that real life always seems to undermine our finely laid-out plans. The phone rings. You have unexpected guests. Projects take twice as long as you anticipate. When we try to fill our schedule too full we set ourselves up for disappointment. That is one of the reasons why I recommend that you cut two activities for every one you add.

This step is similar to the "be flexible" recommendation found in time management books, but with one key exception. Instead of being flexible primarily for ourselves or for others, we are to be flexible so we can be open to God's leading. Don't think that God doesn't care about leading you in your day-to-day life. In Jeremiah 10:23 the author prays, "I know, O Lord, that a man's life is not his own; it is not for man to direct his steps." Proverbs 16:9 states, "In his heart a man plans his course, but the Lord determines his steps."

The funny thing about God's will is that He doesn't map out for us what He wants us to do six months in advance so we can squeeze Him onto our calendars. He wants us to come to Him on our knees each day with expectant hearts, ready to spend the day doing whatever He asks of us. The more we are able to depend on His leading instead of our own obsessive planning, the more we will experience peace and rest on a daily basis. According to Tim Hansel, we will also find that we have enough time to do everything that is important. "As we move closer to God's rhythm for our lives, we realize that he has given us exactly enough time to achieve his purpose for us." [8]

Next Step

Before reading the next chapter, spend some time going through the five steps outlined in the chapter. Ponder the question: What one additional thing could I do that would make the greatest difference in my personal or professional life?

Notes:

1. Charles E. Hummel, *Freedom from Tyranny of the Urgent* (Downers Grove, Illinois: InterVarsity Press, 1997), p. 10.

2. Stephen R. Covey, A. Roger Merrill, and Rebecca R. Merrill, *First Things First* (New York: Simon & Schuster, 1994), p. 37.

3. Ibid., p. 218.

4. Charles E. Hummel, p. 37.

5. Ted W. Engstrom and David J. Juroe, *The Work Trap* (Old Tappan, New Jersey: Fleming H. Revell), 1979, p. 192.

6. Dr. Robert Hemfelt, Dr. Frank Minirth, and Dr. Paul Meier, *We Are Driven* (Carmel, New York: Guideposts, 1991), pp. 70-71.

7. This question is similar to those asked by Stephen R. Covey in his book *7 Habits of Highly Effective People* (New York: Simon & Schuster, 1989), p. 146.

8. Tim Hansel, *When I Relax I Feel Guilty* (Colorado Springs: Chariot Victor Publishing, 1979), p. 69.

Chapter 9

Find Your Daily Rest in Jesus

Wayne knocked on the front door and then looked at his watch. Yes, he had arrived promptly at 7 A.M., just as he promised. Julie opened the door and his face lit up. Her smile instantly made him feel warm all over. "How's the love of my life?" Wayne asked.

Julie tried to answer his question as they walked to the car, but Wayne's mind was already somewhere else, racing with thoughts of the day ahead. He had loads of stuff to do, but he was certain he could squeeze everything in if he timed it all perfectly. He always did.

"Honey, do we have time to stop for breakfast?"

Wayne glanced at his watch and shook his head. "Sorry, I have an early meeting this morning. Looks like today we'll have to settle for fast-food coffee through the drive-up window."

"You mean like we've done all week?"

Even though he could sense some resentment in Julie's voice, Wayne thought he had been successful in fitting his fiancée into a hectic schedule. Taking her to work every day was a great way to spend some time with her, even though she worked just five minutes away from her apartment.

"Are you picking me up, or am I taking the bus home again?" Julie asked, once again interrupting his train of thought.

"I've got meetings running well into the evening. Sorry."

"Well, are we finally going to spend some real time together this weekend? Last weekend you were working and hanging out with your friends."

Wayne made a quick mental note of his schedule, then looked into Julie's eyes. *"I always find time for the one I love. Um . . . how about church on Sunday?"*

How many of you predict a long and happy married life for Wayne and Julie? I'm sure many of you doubt the sincerity of Wayne's expressions of love for his fiancée. If he really loves her, won't he make more time for her in his schedule? Wouldn't he want to spend every available minute with someone who is the love of his life?

The moral of the story is clear: important relationships require time to develop and thrive. Should our relationship with God be any different? Surveys indicate that two out of every three adults in the United States claim to have made a "personal commitment" to Jesus Christ. The same survey and others like it indicate that those who pray do so, on average, for about five minutes a day.[1]

Now there is nothing wrong with five-minute prayers, but no significant relationship, human or divine, can survive solely on a steady diet of miniencounters. When we don't spend more than a few minutes alone with God, we are like Wayne in his treatment of Julie. Like human relationships, our relationship with God is on shaky ground when we consistently ignore Him in favor of other pursuits. Jonathan Edwards, an eighteenth-century pastor who helped bring about America's first Great Awakening, puts it more pointedly: "How can you expect to dwell with God forever, if you so neglect and forsake him here?"[2]

In chapter 7, you read about the rest benefits of a relationship with Jesus Christ. This chapter is on prayer, which I believe is one of the primary means of gaining and securing those benefits. If you have made a commitment to follow Jesus Christ and you feel none of the peace, contentment, and light burdens that Jesus promises, your prayer life is probably the first area to examine.

Perhaps you're saying to yourself that you have "tried prayer," and it didn't produce results as wonderful as I am suggesting. Any brief experiment with prayer is going to have limited success, because prayer is largely a learned activity, and that learning process lasts a lifetime. Rest-producing prayer is different from the "now I lay me down to sleep" poem you might have recited as a child. It also differs from the "drive-up window" prayers we have prayed all too often, where we come to God on the run, dump off our requests, and hit the road again—just as if we were ordering hamburgers.

If you struggle with prayer, don't be discouraged. You are very much in the majority. In fact, Gordon MacDonald believes regular, disciplined prayer to be "one of the most difficult exercises Christians undertake." [3]

Of all the topics I teach and write about, prayer seems to create the most personal discomfort. Oh, it's not a problem with my research or knowledge about prayer—at least not directly. The research did, however, put me in touch with the prayer lives of great saints God has mightily used throughout history. One fact stood out in those stories: the length of time each person spent in prayer. Their daily prayer time wasn't measured in minutes but hours.

My current daily prayer time looks pathetic compared to the two hours spent by John Wesley or the three hours logged in by Martin Luther. I am gaining on them, however. I find it more comforting to look for progress in my prayer life instead of being angry with myself for falling short of history's great prayer warriors. I write these words to you at the age of forty and, right now, I look like Martin Luther compared to my prayer habits at age twenty. I pray that I will be able to say the same thing at age sixty about my current devotional discipline.

Since prayer is too vast a topic to cover in a few pages, this chapter will focus less on technique and more on the need for prayer and its rest benefits. I will also include a few pointers to help make your time in prayer more fruitful.

How Prayer Can Provide Us Rest

In the Bible, it is clear from the start that a weekly Sabbath was a central part of God's provision for rest. The quiet time we spend alone with

God in prayer can supplement the weekly work stoppage, playing the role of a daily Sabbath. Let's look at a few ways that prayer can increase our rest.

Prayer builds our relationship with God. As we have already discussed, relationships grow as we devote more time and attention to them. Spending time with God and His Word helps us mature in our faith, which will strengthen many of the relationship rest benefits discussed in chapter 7. As we mature, we will experience more of the power and fruit of the Holy Spirit, as well as more peace and contentment.

Being with God is the essence of true rest. Hebrews 4 contains repeated references to entering God's rest. Ultimately, we enter God's rest after our lives on earth, when we spend eternity with Him. We can experience a taste of that rest to come every time we bow our heads and open our hearts to God in prayer.

Prayer stills and quiets our soul. When we approach the throne of God in prayer, we have the opportunity to experience what David described in Psalm 131:2: "But I have stilled and quieted my soul; like a weaned child with its mother, like a weaned child is my soul within me." Prayer offers us a respite from the noise and rush of the world, so we can quiet ourselves in the presence of God. When I feel that I am running on empty, I like to find a quiet spot in the woods or along the shoreline to spend an extended period alone with God. Those quiet times quickly recharge my energy reserves, plus my mind slows to a pace where I can hear what God is trying to tell me.

Stillness has physical benefits as well. Dr. Archibald Hart recommends that each person spend at least thirty minutes a day in deep relaxation—and quietly resting in God's presence is a great way to do that. When we slow down, we interrupt the harmful chronic flow of adrenaline caused by our hurried lifestyles. [4]

Prayer provides a daily opportunity for us to surrender control. Real rest begins with a total surrender to God. When Jesus invites us to come to Him and find rest for our souls, He is primarily referring to having a relationship with Him. I find that His invitation works on a daily basis as well. If I skip a day of coming to Jesus in prayer, I end up trying to shoulder all of the worries, sins, and burdens that I normally turn over to Him. Problems and crises affect me far worse than normal. At the end of such a prayerless day, I am weary because I refused to surrender control of the day to Jesus.

In our culture, few people want to surrender control. We are afraid to trust someone who might not look out for our interests as much as we do. God, on the other hand, loves us more than we could ever love ourselves. As an all-knowing God, He can look out for our best interests infinitely better than we can. He is the only One worthy of our surrendering of control.

When we trust God and surrender our lives to Him, He is willing to take all our cares and anxieties, replacing them with His peace. Psalm 55:22 instructs, "Cast your cares on the Lord and he will sustain you." First Peter 5:7 echoes the command, "Cast all your anxiety on him because he cares for you."

Prayer gives us access to divine wisdom and guidance. If you are like me, you might look back on some of the decisions of your youth, shake your head, and say to yourself, "If only I had known then what I know now." Fortunately, God does not want us to always learn our lessons the hard way. He desires to give us wisdom beyond our years. I find James 1:5 particularly encouraging: "If any of you lacks wisdom, he should ask God, who gives generously to all without finding fault, and it will be given to him."

Through prayer, the Bible, and other mature Christians, God is able to provide guidance to help us through even the most difficult of decisions. The chronicles of Jesus' ministry seem to indicate that the more pressing the situation He faced, the more time He spent in prayer. When Jesus chose the twelve apostles, the men who would be the foundation for His church, He spent the whole night before the decision in prayer (see Luke 6:12-13). If the Son of God sees fit to pull an all-nighter with His Father before a major decision, perhaps we need to spend more than five minutes consulting with God for our own choices.

How does this divine guidance produce rest? First, when we are confident of the rightness of our choice, we find a certain peace about the decision. We are no longer fretting over the alternatives, anxious about making a wrong move. For example, once I discovered the type of work God had called me to do, anxieties over my career direction virtually disappeared.

The other way God's guidance produces rest is by helping us focus on what is most important. When I have a sense of what God wants me to do, I prioritize better, meaning I tend to eliminate more trivial matters from my calendar. A less-cluttered schedule provides me with more time for rest and relaxation.

Prayer allows God to work through us with His power. We grow weary when we pile our schedules full of the things we think we ought to do, without pausing to let God shape our plans. We then ask God to bless our plans, which in essence is saying, "My will be done," instead of "Thy will be done." This is wrong. We are not meant to go off on our own to do a bunch of stuff, even if much of that stuff is for God. Our task is to be available to let God work in His power through us.

Jesus promised His followers "power" when they received the Holy Spirit in Acts 1:8. In John 15:5, Jesus refers to Himself as the vine and us as the branches. If we remain "in" Him our lives will bear much fruit, but apart from Him we "can do nothing." The way we best stay "in" Jesus is to develop the relationship through prayer. His will is for each of us to bear fruit in our lives, and He promises to put His power to work in accomplishing that. Our task is to keep our attention on Him and follow His leading. Nothing keeps our attention on God as much as prayer. According to Bill Hybels, pastor of Willow Creek Community Church, "Prayer is the key to unlocking God's prevailing power in your life." [5]

A Quiet Approach to Prayer

When I was younger, I was able to get through my prayers in rapid fashion. I rattled on with quick words of praise to God, then confessed my sins, listed off some things for which I was thankful, then presented my requests—for me and for others. When I ran out of things to say, I concluded with "in Jesus' name I pray. Amen."

I did not need to slow down to go through these prayers. Frequently, I prayed them while driving to work. When I was done, I felt a little better, but I couldn't say I felt much closer to God as a result. I had merely fulfilled my obligation.

My prayer life began to change back in 1988, when I first participated in a silent retreat. I found my old prayer style did not last me long into the retreat. I eventually ran out of things to say to God during those three days, so I stayed silent and waited to see if He had anything to say to me. He did. When I finally quieted my mind, it allowed me to pick up His thoughts and instructions for me. Much of the teaching and writing I have done during the past decade have been inspired through these extended silent times with God.

Although I frequently fall back into my old habits, each year my prayer time contains less talk and more silence. For the remainder of the chapter, I will share the approach to prayer I currently use. It is intended as an illustration to give you ideas for your own prayer time, not as a format to follow religiously (I don't even do this every day). The approach is hardly an original one; most of the literature on prayer includes guidelines strikingly similar to mine, which is understandable since those writings have influenced the way I pray.

• **Read from the Bible.** I generally start my time with God by opening the Bible. Second Timothy 3:16-17 best describes the value of God's Word: "All Scripture is God-breathed and is useful for teaching, rebuking, correcting and training in righteousness, so that the man of God may be thoroughly equipped for every good work." Nearly every person in the United States owns at least one Bible, but I encounter frighteningly few Christians who have read it from cover to cover. People excuse their ignorance by saying that hardly anyone reads books these days. I don't think God would see that excuse as valid. After all, if God didn't intend people to read, then why did He make the Bible so long?

I generally read from five minutes to fifteen minutes of Scripture every day. I tend to go through the Bible from beginning to end every two years—although I hope to improve upon that. My own Bible reading habits look pitiful compared to others I've read about who get through the Bible once, twice, or even four times a year. If we believe the Bible to be God's Word and a useful guide for living, then we should spend at least as much time with it as we do with newspapers, magazines, popular fiction, or on-line reading.

• **Meditate on God's Word.** This is a practice I have not done with regularity until recently. To most people, meditation conjures up images of Eastern mysticism and people dressed in white humming out their mantra. Those people don't realize that meditation is something God's people have practiced for thousands of years. In fact, the more I read on prayer, the more I learn that meditation is not just a useful activity, but a necessary one. Donald Whitney calls meditation on Scripture "the missing link between Bible intake and prayer," meaning it helps us shift our focus from the printed page to the Living God. [6]

Basically, meditation on Scripture means to silently ponder it, thinking about what the passages say about God and what they say to you. Richard Foster points out that meditation differs from scholarly study of Scripture in that it "centers on internalizing and personalizing the passage. The written Word becomes a living word addressed to you." [7]

A person can meditate on any piece of Scripture, from something as short as a single word or as long as a chapter or two. Those just starting out might want to begin with something from Psalms or Proverbs. Let me illustrate using a passage familiar to many, Proverbs 3:5-6: "Trust in the Lord with all your heart and lean not on your own understanding; in all your ways acknowledge him, and he will make your paths straight."

What does this passage say about God? For starters, it says we should trust Him and, if we acknowledge Him in all our ways, He will keep our lives on the right path. Those thoughts should lead us to praise and thank God. Then we need to turn to ourselves. Do I trust God? What does "all your heart" mean and do I trust Him in that way? What kind of troubles have I gotten into by leaning on my own understanding? How can I acknowledge God in all my ways? Do I face issues in my life where finding a "straight path" would be welcome?

As you can see from this example, a little pondering on this passage from Proverbs can provide a wealth of material for one's prayer time. In fact, you will probably find yourself bouncing back and forth between silent meditation and praying to God. Let the passage take you anywhere the Holy Spirit moves you.

• **Adore and praise God.** The next four elements of prayer I learned back in college from a little pamphlet published by NavPress entitled "Seven Minutes with God: How to Plan a Daily Quiet Time." Robert Foster outlines a four-step process that is easy to remember because it spells out the word ACTS: adoration, confession, thanksgiving, and supplication.

Adoration is simply praising God. We might tell Him how much we love Him or reflect upon His goodness, power, or love. We might sing a song of worship to Him or read a Psalm that is addressed to God. Adoration is effective in taking our attention away from our self-centered thoughts and directing it toward God.

• **Confess our sins.** I don't know too many people who enjoy confessing their sins to God, but it is necessary. When we list our sins to God, we are not telling Him anything new. He knows about all our sinful thoughts and deeds. He wants us to agree with Him that they are sinful and ask His forgiveness. When God forgives sins, He wipes the slate clean of the dirt and clutter that hinder our communication with Him. God is now ready to listen to our requests and we are now in a position to listen to Him.

• **Thank Him for all He is and does.** First Thessalonians 5:16-18 provides great instruction for praying Christians: "Be joyful always; pray continually; give thanks in all circumstances, for this is God's will for you in Christ Jesus." Even though I discussed this passage in the chapter on contentment, it bears repeating. Notice the strong words: *always, continually, all.* This command flies in the face of our normal behavior. We tend to be joyful only when everything is going our way (i.e., never), pray when we need something, give thanks during good times, and complain to God when times are tough. God's will for us is that joy, prayer, and thankfulness become a constant in our lives, instead of the exception.

The other important point to take from this passage is this: God has given us things to be thankful for no matter what circumstances we face. We tend to focus on what is imperfect in our lives. God wants us to focus on the blessings He has provided. For patients who feel overwhelmed by their problems, the doctors of the Minirth-Meier Clinic have long prescribed making lists of everything positive for which they are thankful. Some patients even create permanent "blessing" journals that they are to review regularly. If you have trouble feeling thankful for anything, this practice might prove especially fruitful. [8]

• **Lift up your supplications.** I almost decided to use the word request in place of supplication, since it is a more familiar term. Then I checked the dictionary. Supplicate means to ask humbly and earnestly. That is a perfect description of how our requests should be presented to God.

What should we ask for? If you can't answer the question by this point in your time of prayer, I recommend waiting in silence until the Holy Spirit provides some guidance. I usually pray for other people before I include my own requests. I give special attention to those I know who are trying to live their lives apart from God. This is also a good time to turn over to God all your areas of fear and worry. Ask Him to guide you in what you are to do today and to keep you from worrying about tomorrow.

• **Wait and listen for God's answers and/or instruction.** "Be still, and know that I am God." Those instructions from Psalm 46:10 have had a profound influence on my prayer life. The most restful time I spend with God is when I sit still and silent, being aware of little else except for being in His presence. This is the time He encourages me and lifts my spirits. This is also when He convicts me of what I need to do or what I need to change in my life. When I am still long enough, He almost always speaks, not in a voice my ears hear but one that my heart and mind can clearly distinguish.

Even though this aspect of prayer is listed last, it is perhaps the most critical component for those of you in desperate need of rest. Silence and stillness in the presence of God is the most authentic rest one can experience in this life. He alone can restore strength in your body, mind, heart, and soul.

Next Step

If you do not have a regular time of prayer, commit to spending at least thirty minutes in prayer tomorrow. Perhaps you can go to bed earlier tonight so you can get up earlier in the morning for prayer. Whatever format you follow for prayer, try to spend at least ten minutes in silence, either listening or meditating on God's Word. Each month, see if you can add five additional minutes to your daily prayer sessions.

Notes:

1. The surveys I referred to were cited in the following two sources: George Barna, *The Index of Leading Spiritual Indicators* (Dallas: Word Publishing, 1996), pp. 3, 61; Donald S. Whitney, *Spiritual Disciplines for the Christian Life* (Colorado Springs: NavPress, 1991), p. 62.

2. Jonathan Edwards, "Hypocrites Deficient in the Duty of Prayer," *The Works of Jonathan Edwards* (Peabody, Massachusetts: Hendrickson Publishers, Inc., 1998), Vol. 2, p. 75.

3. Gordon MacDonald, *Ordering Your Private World* (Nashville: Thomas Nelson Publishers, 1984), p. 156.

4. Dr. Archibald D. Hart, *The Hidden Link Between Adrenalin and Stress* (Dallas: Word Publishing, 1991), p. 148.

5. Bill Hybels, *Too Busy Not to Pray* (Downers Grove, Illinois: InterVarsity Press, 1988), p. 13.

6. Whitney, p. 67.

7. Richard J. Foster, *Celebration of Discipline* (San Francisco: Harper & Row, Publishers, 1978), p. 20.

8. Frank Minirth, Paul Meier, Don Hawkins, Chris Thurman, and Richard Flournoy, *Beating Burnout* (New York: Inspirational Press, 1997), p. 323.

Chapter 10

Rediscover the Sabbath

B art opened the door to his office and flipped on the lights and his computer. This was his favorite time of the week, 6 A.M. Monday morning, when he got a jump on the competition while they were still in their bathrobes. That his was the only light on in the building confirmed Bart's elite status—at least in his own mind.

He jotted down a handful of voice-mail messages and then eased up to the computer screen to check his e-mail. Since yesterday was spent at home doing paperwork—his wife complained when he spent every day at the office—the mailbox would be bursting with messages. After taking an hour to respond to the usual round of requests, Bart noticed a strange message title. All it said was, "A message from God."

Hmm, Bart thought. Probably one of those crank e-mails people feel they need to forward to everyone in their address book. He hoped it didn't contain a virus, like the computer equivalent of Armageddon. Even though this couldn't have anything to do with work, he had to check it out. The message read:

"Dear Bart:

"I have wanted to get through to you for a while now, so I thought I'd use the only medium you seem to check and respond to with any regularity.

"Yes, this really is a message from God, the One in whom you say you believe. You made a commitment to Me years ago but, since then, you never slow down long enough for us to communicate. Oh sure, you squeeze in a quick 'Bless this day, Lord' in the morning, then hit the ground running before giving Me a chance to respond.

"I know how much time it takes to work in today's marketplace, but you spend nearly every waking moment working or thinking about your work. You have performed some amazing feats during your seven-day workweeks, but if you'd stop and listen to Me you could accomplish things of more lasting value.

"Bart, why are you unwilling to participate in My holy day of rest each week? That's right, I made the day I rested the holy day, not the six days I worked. I know you say that rest is only for the weak, and you'll resort to rest when you just can't work any longer. Think about this: Do I, God, need to rest? I did not rest on the seventh day because I needed to, but because I wanted to create holy time in the week and provide an example for you and others to follow. Rest is a holy activity.

"Take yesterday for instance. You may have been able to fool your wife, but I know what you're up to. I know that you asked a coworker to call you up on a Sunday morning to go over a report, just so you could work while your family was at church. Then, although you pretended to be lounging in your recliner, you were actually doing office paperwork all afternoon. Going out to dinner with an important client made a perfect ending to a completely restless day.

"Next week, I'd like you to try to create a real Sabbath day of rest. All I require is that you do no work of any kind and spend at least a little of that time with Me for a change. Instead of paperwork or household chores, how about having a talk with your wife or playing with your children? You'll be amazed at the difference this kind of day will make. You might even slow down long enough to hear something from Me. How about it?

"I look forward to spending the time with you."

If God made a habit of taking this approach in His communication with us, I think we'd all find some additional messages in our various "in" boxes. I know I would have amassed quite a collection over the years. God doesn't usually communicate this way, however. Most of the time, He waits for us to slow down and quiet down enough to perceive what He is trying to tell us. Some of us, like Bart, never slow down enough for something like that to happen.

Writing about the Sabbath is a challenge. Of all the Ten Commandments, this one is probably the most misunderstood, misused, and widely ignored. Some have turned the Sabbath into a glum, burdensome day filled with do's and don'ts, while others sprint through the day as if it were like any other on the treadmill of life. Both approaches do a disservice to God's Sabbath commandment and contribute to the general restlessness of our culture.

In this chapter, I hope to cut through some of the mistaken notions and traditions of Sabbath and present the biblical basics on the subject. As we gain a better understanding of why God created the Sabbath for us, we might actually desire to observe it, instead of participating out of a sense of obligation or guilt. I will also provide a look at some of the possibilities for creating a restful Sabbath, being careful not to create a new list of do's and don'ts.

What God Values in the Sabbath

Resting every seventh day is not some outdated portion of Old Testament law. The cycle of work and rest has been present from the beginning, when God created the world in six days and rested on the seventh. As I noted in chapter 2, the Creation account found in the Book of Genesis indicates that God blessed the seventh day and made it holy because it was the day He rested from His work. Thus, from the beginning, rest has been deemed a holy activity by God. Those who have felt too guilty to stop their busyness, take note: *Rest is holy.*

In my search through the Bible, I could only find one "do" and one "don't" regarding the Sabbath. The one thing we are told to do is to gather together to worship God. The one thing God rules out for us on the Sabbath is work of any kind. Other than those commands, God has given us great freedom in experiencing our day of rest.

Leviticus 23:3 refers to the Sabbath as "a day of sacred assembly."

Finding Rest When the Work Is Never Done

One day a week we are to gather to worship and give thanks to our Lord and God. The Jews have traditionally celebrated the Sabbath on the seventh day, which on our current calendar is Saturday. Early Christians added an assembly celebrating the resurrection of Jesus on what is now Sunday, the first day of the week. Several hundred years later, Christian churches combined the two into a Sunday Sabbath. Although some still argue as to which day of the week to keep the Sabbath, the Bible is clear that we are to set aside one day each week to gather with others to worship God.

Although church attendance figures suggest that many in our culture do not regularly assemble to worship God, it is not the most glaring violation of the Sabbath commandment. The most ignored aspect of the Sabbath is the command to "not do any work." In our hyperactive society, it is difficult to find any "responsible" person who can go an entire day without doing any work. We are all much too busy for that.

During my early adult years, I viewed the Sabbath as more of a slowing-down day than a day of rest. Since Monday was the day I prepared my weekly to-do list, Sunday became my last chance to check off those tasks that remained undone. I rarely did work for my employer, but I often used the time to catch up on household chores or homework if I was taking or teaching a class. It was a slower-paced day, but hardly a day of rest.

As I studied God's Word concerning the Sabbath, I realized how poorly I was honoring this holy day. The commandment to keep the Sabbath holy is included in the same Ten Commandments as "thou shall not kill"—and its violation was also punishable by death under the Law (Exodus 31:15; 35:2). Keeping one day set aside for rest and worship is something God did in creating the world, as an example for us to follow. It is part of a sacred rhythm of work and rest that we violate at our own peril.

Because Jesus was accused of violating some of the additional burdensome Sabbath requirements imposed by the Pharisees, it is possible for us to think He did not consider the Sabbath important. Yet, throughout the New Testament, we see no evidence of Jesus violating this commandment, and in Luke 23:56, His followers were said to have rested on the Sabbath. In defending His so-called Sabbath violations to the Pharisees in Mark 2:27, Jesus said, "The Sabbath was made for man, not man for the Sabbath."

What did Jesus mean when He said that the Sabbath was "made for man"? God did not create the Sabbath as a sinister device aimed at wiping out the last trace of pleasure from our lives. On the contrary, the Sabbath was made for us, meaning God intended it for our benefit. Although a day of rest may seem to have little value by the world's measurements, it is of great value to God. Let's take a look at some of the valuable aspects of Sabbath rest:

• **Contemplation.** Most days we tend to place a greater emphasis on doing than thinking. Besides doing, God wants His children to be wise and "give thought to their ways" (Proverbs 14:8). Wayne Muller calls the Sabbath "an incubator for wisdom" because the removal of rush and pressure allows us to see things more clearly. [1]

• **Evaluation.** During the Creation account, God periodically stepped back from His work and noted that "it was good." When we stop to assess our efforts, it allows us to celebrate our successes and learn from our mistakes. In my own case, I find such an evaluation gives me a renewed sense of what is important, which helps me make better use of my time.

• **Restoration.** Rest is part of the word restoration, which means that it restores to us what the previous week of activity has taken out of us. Without this restoring pause, we end up wearing down and burning out. On the Sabbath we can also experience restoration in our relationship with God. Sometimes I get too caught up in my own agenda during the work week, but through worship and prayer on the Sabbath, I return God to His rightful place on the throne of my heart.

• **Celebration.** The Sabbath is not to be a day of drudgery and deprivation. In Exodus 31:16 the Israelites are instructed to celebrate the Sabbath. Isaiah 58:13-14 uses words like delight and joy in connection with keeping the Sabbath. This is to be a day of smiling, not frowning. Marva Dawn, in her book *Keeping the Sabbath Wholly*, does a beautiful job of describing how to celebrate a Sabbath:

> Most of the days of the week we do what we have to do, what is expected of us. Sabbath keeping frees us to take delight in everything, to uncork our own spontaneity. Because there is nothing we *have* to do, we are free suddenly to say yes to invitations, to read fairy tales, to be children, to discover the presence of God hidden all around us. To keep the Sabbath invites us to have festival fun, to play, to enjoy our guests and our activities, to relish the opportunity for worship, to celebrate the eternal presence of God himself. [2]

• **Inspiration.** In the last chapter, we discussed the importance of slowing down and being silent so God can communicate with us. If you are like me, you understand how challenging it is to slow down, for most of us live as if striding down a long people-mover, those horizontal escalators found in airports that are designed to whisk you from one end of the concourse to another. I never realize how fast I am going on those overgrown treadmills, until I reach solid ground at the end and stumble because my feet can no longer keep up with my body. A day of rest allows us to noticeably slow down so we can get in step with God. When I halt the sprint of life and set aside my agenda for a day, quite often God begins to share His agenda with me.

• **Separation.** God knows that we take ourselves too seriously. He knows we get caught up in our work and think things won't get done if we don't do them. He also knows that we have a tendency to get caught up in the world's values, in all the gold and glitter it has to offer. I think these are the sort of things God is referring to in Isaiah 58:13-14 when He tells the Israelites they will find joy if they honor the Sabbath "by not going your own way and not doing as you please or speaking idle words." The Sabbath provides us an opportunity to separate ourselves from our worldly influenced ways and let God guide us gently back on track, so we can experience joy instead of just stress.

• **Communion.** I am not referring specifically to the remembrance of Holy Communion, but to the intimate sharing and fellowship with others that the word suggests. Deep relationships, the kind that make life exciting and joyful, take time to develop. During the week, our to-do lists of tasks often win out over time with people and time with God. When we set aside those tasks on the Sabbath, we are free to enjoy our significant relationships without fretting over what is being neglected on our schedules. I love Sabbath day conversations with others, because I know I don't have to cut them short because of something else I have to do.

Freedom from "Ought to"

How do we observe the Sabbath without creating a day so filled with do's and don'ts that we wind up exhausted and glad to have the day end? What I've found helpful is to avoid viewing the Sabbath as one more to-do item on my week's list. My Sabbath becomes more restful when I approach it as a day of freedom from all the other "ought to's" in my life. I worship God, shelve all my projects, then relax and enjoy what the day brings.

Since the Bible provides only minimal guidelines for Sabbath keeping, it is important that we not burden ourselves and others with additional requirements for the day. The Jews have a list of thirty-nine prohibitions against work on the Sabbath, but I haven't felt the need to consult it to see whether I am working or not. I also try not to appoint myself judge in terms of how others observe the Sabbath, which means I don't yell at fellow Christians who pull a few weeds from their garden or don't attend every single church event on Sunday.

Without creating more rules, is there any valid criteria for evaluating what we do or do not do on the Sabbath? In my own practice, I've found it helpful to ask myself these two questions:
• Will this help turn my attention and focus to God?
• Will this help me become more rested and refreshed?
When faced with a potential Sabbath "activity," I feel good about pursuing it if I can answer yes to at least one of these questions. Worship, prayer, and Scripture reading are good examples of "yes" answers to the first question. A nap or a walk with my wife on the beach would receive "yes" answers to question number two. Sometimes the intensity

of the activity makes a difference in my answer. I would say yes to casually shooting a basketball with friends in our driveway but no to a three-on-three full-court game.

In a manner similar to my personal criteria, pastor and author Eugene Peterson reduces the Sabbath essentials down to two words: praying and playing. He stresses that both are critical practices:

> Both playing and praying, praying and playing, are essential for good Sabbath keeping. A Sabbath that omits one or the other is not a true Sabbath. But it is difficult to integrate them. Our commonest experience is with their separation. In America we have conspicuous examples of widespread observance of half-Sabbaths, prayerful Sabbaths without any play, and playful Sabbaths without any prayer. Our Puritan ancestors practiced the first; our pagan contemporaries practice the second. [3]

What Do I Do on a Day of Rest?

In my research on the Sabbath, I discovered a history filled with half-Sabbath keeping. Because of this history, I have found many people who believe the Sabbath is not for them. The most common objection I hear to rest—particularly Sabbath rest—comes from those who tell me they can't "just sit around and do nothing." I have two responses to that comment.

First, a day of rest does not mean sitting lifeless from dawn to dusk. To do this would make the Pharisees of Jesus' time look lax by comparison. There is some middle ground between a day of motionless boredom and one jammed with nonstop activity.

My second response to those who can't just sit around and do nothing is a question: Why not? Why can't you sit quietly on the front porch with a glass of lemonade and enjoy a beautiful afternoon? Why can't you sit on a park bench with someone you love and just talk? Why can't you turn off the television and CD player for a few hours and enjoy the silence? Can you obey God's command to "be still and know that I am God?" If you find it impossible to simply sit and do nothing for even thirty minutes, you may have just passed the test to join the growing ranks of activity addicts.

Besides nothing, what else might one do on a Sabbath day of rest? My best advice is to experiment until you find out what works for you. Here are some things that have worked well for me.

• **Enjoy God's creation.** Whether it be in the wilderness, a neighborhood park, or your own backyard garden, take some time to "stop and smell the roses." As we enjoy what God has made, it often becomes a time of praise and prayer. Wayne Muller calls time in nature "the most nourishing, healing Sabbath practice." [4]

• **Ignore your calendar, planner, and/or to-do lists.** For better or for worse, I am a constant planner and list maker—except on the Sabbath. In order to make that day a definite break from my normal routine, I rarely plan the day and never make a list. It is my day to be spontaneous. If Kathy and I are enjoying talking to friends after church, our schedule is usually free to say, "Hey, how about lunch?" For me, freedom from planning is very restful.

• **Take a nap.** When was the last time you took a nap? Falling asleep on the sofa while watching television doesn't count. I am not normally a nap taker—I think I once lasted an entire decade without one—but I find it refreshing, particularly on days when I am dragging and could use the extra sleep. I know of one family that set aside two hours every Sunday afternoon for taking a nap. Over time, friends knew that this was not a time for them to call or stop by. This practice enables everyone in the family to experience extra physical rest each week in addition to the spiritual rest of Sunday worship.

• **Gather for a feast.** If any of you have hosted an elaborate dinner party, you might be skeptical about feasting on a day set apart for rest. When I advocate a feast, I do not mean a meal where the hosts spend the entire day in the kitchen and wind up exhausted. The point of a feast is to gather with friends and family to celebrate the Sabbath and each other. If you limit yourself to foods that can be prepared the day before and refrigerated or reheated, you will be able to pay attention to the people instead of the preparations. Some of my fondest memories of times with friends include lunch or dinner gatherings when the conversation lasted hours longer than the food.

• **Enjoy extended time with God.** During the week it is always a challenge to carve out an adequate chunk of time to spend with God. Even as we read the Bible or pray, we often find ourselves distracted with thoughts of all that needs doing. On a day when nothing has to be done, we can enjoy a lengthy rest in God's presence instead of our normal practice of praying on the run.

• **Take a day off from your computer or television.** The Sabbath commandments of the Old Testament specify rest for everyone in the household, including servants and livestock (see Exodus 23:12). Although our appliances don't need rest in the same way living beings do, I think it is difficult to experience much rest in a household where the computer, stereo, telephone, washing machine, and television are all in constant use. Make a family decision to limit or omit a couple of those appliances for the day. In the past, I have spent the bulk of my Sabbath days in front of the television and, believe me, it did not bring me even a shred of rest. Don't be too rigid with this suggestion, though, like deciding to cut out television on Super Bowl Sunday.

• **Look over your work and see the good in it.** Just as God looked over His work of creation and saw that it was good, we can benefit from looking back at our own efforts. Take something you have worked hard on or feel good about and pause to look over your endeavors. This pause can relate to your work, your family or even your favorite hobby. As I write this, the gardens around our neighborhood are in full summer bloom. Those who have labored so hard to make their gardens beautiful would find it greatly rewarding to take an afternoon to simply gaze out and appreciate the colors.

For those of you who haven't had time for Sabbath rest, I ask you to try it for a month. You are likely to discover the same secret I learned: there is no sacrifice to Sabbath rest. My day of freedom from the grind so rejuvenates me, I find I can accomplish more of value in six days than I used to do in seven. Learn to stop for rest on your own, before the pace of life forces rest upon you.

Next Step

Within the next seven days, give yourself a Sabbath. If you are part of the burgeoning weekend workforce, your day off may not coincide with a church worship service. In that case, you might want to begin your Sabbath with your own private worship service. At the end of the day, take a few minutes to reflect on how you feel. Did you find time to get close to God? Do you feel a little more rested to tackle the coming week? Think about what you can do on the next Sabbath to improve your answers to those questions.

Notes:

1. Wayne Muller, *Sabbath: Restoring the Sacred Rhythm of Rest* (New York: Bantam Books, 1999), p. 165.
2. Marva J. Dawn, *Keeping the Sabbath Wholly* (Grand Rapids, Michigan: William B. Eerdmans Publishing Company, 1989), p. 202.
3. Eugene H. Peterson, "Confessions of a Former Sabbath Breaker," *Christianity Today*, September 2, 1988, p. 28.
4. Muller, p. 80.

Chapter 11

Restore Rest through Retreat

Before the age of twenty-nine, I thought I had experienced retreat and extended time alone with God. After all, I was a veteran of a number of church retreats, plus I had enjoyed several partial-day prayer sessions walking in the woods.

In early April of 1988, I left behind a hectic day of work and drove a short distance to a retreat center located on the shore of a quiet lake east of town. The extra push at work would be worth it, I felt, because I had three days to be with God, plus an upcoming week of vacation. I knew only one of the sixty or so men on the retreat, a coworker who had recommended the place to me. That didn't bother me much, since all but an hour of each day would be spent in silence.

With most of us still in suits from the workweek, we had dinner, then sat through a brief program explaining the rules of the retreat. After that, we entered the sanctuary to begin our worship service and our time of silence. I had never been silent in a group of people before, so it was an unusual but calming experience. I didn't need to focus on making small talk, which meant I could better concentrate on God.

After worship, I returned to my room with excitement, eager to dig into the reading I had brought, eager to start three days of praying. Within minutes I was sound asleep.

I woke early on Friday, as I usually do when I sleep away from home. I was able to pray for a few moments in my room before heading off to the Scripture service. Breakfast was eaten in silence, except for a taped lesson coming over the speakers and the clanging of cups and forks.

After the morning session, I explored the expansive grounds of the retreat center and reflected on what I had heard and read. It was delightful to be in prayer without feeling rushed, knowing I still had more than two days left before I rejoined the rest of the world.

When we finished with lunch, we retreated to our rooms for a one-hour rest period. I hadn't taken a nap (intentionally) since I was a child, so I approached the time with skepticism. I dutifully retired to the bed in my room, while my mind raced with thoughts of more "spiritual" activities I should be pursuing.

The next thing I remember was the ringing of the wake-up bell. I hadn't slept for long, but once I got through a few minutes of grogginess, I felt refreshed. By the third day this became one of my favorite parts of the retreat.

The first day brought more sessions and readings to ponder, more silent meals, and more walks through the surrounding woods and fields. I noticed my internal clock slowing down as the day progressed. It became easier for me to sort out difficult spiritual concepts at this pace. For example, the book I had brought to read besides the Bible was Thoughts in Solitude by Thomas Merton. I had attempted to start the book several times in the past, without much success. I guess it took solitude to put my mind in the proper mode to read about the subject.

As the retreat wore on, I moved from resting in God's presence and enjoying His creation to reflecting on my everyday service to Him. I pondered what it meant to serve God "full time" and yet not occupy the position of pastor or missionary. I evaluated my walk with God thus far and began to receive insights on how I could grow and serve Him better.

I decided that if I was committed to God, all my desires and actions should center on Him. In that vein, I was convicted to keep more alert to ministry opportunities that God may present to me—and vowed to make time for them when they arose.

Saturday ended with me on the shore watching the sun set over the lake. I've always been a fan of sunsets, but I had never before felt the glory of God's creation as intensely as I did that night. The orderly and colorful transition from day to night and the rhythm of waves splashing on the shore filled me with a sense of the completeness of God's work.

Having some idea of what God wanted me to work on, the final day of the retreat was spent simply enjoying God's presence. Two days later, while brainstorming business ideas with a good friend, God provided me with a vision for the ministry opportunities He wanted me to pursue. That vision has been the driving force behind the bulk of my writing, teaching, and business activities ever since.

When you spend an extended period of time alone with God, your life will never be the same. Since that first experience, I have tried to schedule such a retreat every year. Each time I come away profoundly changed.

Before I expound on the rest benefits of a retreat, let me start by clarifying what kind of retreat I will be proposing—or more precisely, not proposing. Some of you may have experienced a church retreat before. In most cases, you drive several hours to the camp or retreat center, stay in rustic accommodations, listen to speakers, eat too much, play games, and try to sleep amidst the snoring of your roommates. Although these retreats can be enjoyable, I've rarely found them to be restful.

Retreats that restore us are simply times of silence and solitude in God's presence. Other than that, the retreat you make could be held either in the city or country, be alone or in a group, be structured or free-flowing. The point is to relax and give our relationship with God the time it deserves.

A retreat offers many of the same rest benefits as the other practices outlined in this section, except it usually provides them in larger doses. If you are observing a weekly Sabbath and daily prayer time but still feel chronically weary, a retreat of three or more days might be just what you need.

Actually, it is best not to wait until you are in dire need of a retreat to schedule one. No room for a retreat on your calendar? That is when you most need to push aside your projects and get away, according to Emilie Griffin, author of *Wilderness Time: A Guide for Spiritual Retreat.* Griffin is not in favor of waiting for free time or special occasions to go on retreat:

> People sometimes suppose that a special reason is needed to justify making a retreat. We assume that a retreat needs to be made on a certain occasion. In fact, no more reason is needed than that your heart longs for greater closeness with God—because you are worn out by many annoyances and worries, and you are seeking the refreshment of God's presence; because you need rest from the anxieties of ordinary living, even from the legitimate responsibilities imposed by family, work, and church; because you want to follow the example of Jesus in going apart to pray. [1]

Jesus in Solitude

The four gospels are filled with wonderful stories of Jesus' life on earth. It is hard for me to forget His great miracles and acts of compassion. The wisdom of His teaching will always give me guidance. Yet, one aspect of the life of Jesus had escaped my attention until recently. I realized that He was a man who frequently left the crowds behind to go off and spend time with His Father.

The ministry of Jesus began with a period of solitude and isolation. After His baptism by John the Baptist, the Holy Spirit led Jesus alone into the desert to be tempted by the devil. For forty days Jesus fasted and prayed. (Although the Scripture references do not specifically mention that He prayed, every other time Jesus went off alone, we are told that He prayed. So it's safe to answer that this forty-day period included praying, too.) At the end of this time, when Jesus was physically the weakest, the devil presented his big three temptations: turn the stones into bread, throw Himself down from the top of the temple, and worship Satan in exchange for all the kingdoms of the world. Jesus, although hungry and weak, was easily up to the spiritual challenge. Although Scripture doesn't fully explain all the reasons for this wilderness encounter, the fact that it occurred immediately before Christ's active ministry suggests that it was necessary preparation for the divine work that was to follow.

As Jesus began preaching and performing miracles, throngs of people crowded around Him to be healed. Yet, Luke 5:16 notes that "Jesus often withdrew to lonely places and prayed." The next chapter of Luke points out that Jesus spent the night before He chose the twelve apostles on a mountainside in prayer. Even the Messiah saw fit to spend extended time with the Father before a major decision.

Later Jesus sent out these same apostles two-by-two to preach and heal in all the villages of Israel. When they returned from their journeys, Jesus told them, "Come with me by yourselves to a quiet place and get some rest" (Mark 6:31). Getting away from the crowds and noise is a means of rest Jesus both practiced and recommended to others.

Solitude can also help us confront life's setbacks. Matthew 14 tells of the beheading of John the Baptist, whose ministry in Israel had been surpassed only by Jesus Himself. Upon hearing of his death, Jesus withdrew privately by boat to a solitary place (verse 13). The crowds—as they often did—discovered His retreat location and He had compassion on them despite His grief. After a miraculous multiplying of the five loaves and two fishes, Jesus dismissed the crowd, put the disciples on a boat, and went up alone on a mountainside to pray. Despite the substantial interruptions of the day, Jesus found time to return to the solitude He desired.

Finally, Jesus spent the final moments of His freedom at a place called Gethsemane, which is thought to have been a garden of sorts located on the Mount of Olives east of Jerusalem. Even though He took the disciples with Him, Jesus went off a little distance from them to pray. He was, for the most part, alone with God in this case as well, since His disciples kept falling asleep. According to Luke 21:37, Jesus spent each night during His last week in Jerusalem somewhere on the Mount of Olives.

What are we to make of this solitary Jesus? Donald Whitney sums it up nicely in *Spiritual Disciplines for the Christian Life*:

Put yourself in Jesus' sandals for a moment. People are clamoring for your help and have many real needs. You are able to meet all those needs. Can you ever feel justified in pulling away [to be] alone? Jesus did. We love to feel wanted. We love the sense of importance/power/indispensability (pick one) that comes from doing something no one else can do. But Jesus did not succumb to those temptations. He knew the importance of disciplining Himself to be alone. By now the point should be obvious: To be like Jesus we must discipline ourselves to find times of silence and solitude. [2]

Why Retreat?

Besides following the example of Jesus, there are several other reasons to invest time in a rest retreat:

• **It will deepen our relationship with Jesus.** Jesus asks us to come into relationship with Him so that He can provide rest for our souls. To build up this kind of relationship, like any other, time is required. E. M. Bounds once wrote, "God's acquaintance is not made by quick visits." [3]

When we pull away from the world for a few days, we finally become available for God to reveal Himself to us, to mold us, and to strengthen us. According to Bill Hybels, this time away is essential for our faith to grow. "No one can become an authentic Christian on a steady diet of activity. Power comes out of stillness; strength comes out of solitude. Decisions that change the entire course of your life come out from the Holy of Holies, your time of stillness before God." [4]

• **We develop more perspective and direction for our lives.** Perspective is hard for me to achieve when my nose is to the grindstone. I find that situations often trouble me because I have not taken the time to step back to reflect and pray. When I retreat from my day-to-day world, I can see everything in my life with a new perspective, one that comes from my time with the One who tells me to trust Him and not worry.

We also need time to sort through our endless pile of tasks and reassess (or assess if we've never done it before) the direction of our lives. When you drive somewhere you haven't been before, what is more important; the speed at which you are driving or good directions to your destination? Until you point the car in the right direction, speed will probably take you further from where you want to go instead of closer. Who better to ask for directions than God? According to Charles Hummel, it is impossible to do God's will if we don't stop to learn what it is:

> Prayerful waiting on God is indispensable to effective service. Here we learn the truth about God, ourselves and the tasks he wants us to undertake. Christians who are too busy to stop, take spiritual inventory and receive their assignments from God may be productive. We may work day and night to achieve much that seems significant to ourselves and to others. But we don't complete the work God has for us to do. [5]

• **We gain the fuel and substance needed for us to serve those we care about.** When my energy reserves are depleted, the needs of others tend to frustrate me because I have little of myself left to share. If I have had little time to think or pray, I find that when I open my mouth, the words that escape are of little value to anyone, including myself. Time away from people and with God helps to create a person who will have more to offer others when he or she returns. I remember hearing my wife, Kathy, talking to another woman about how excited they were about their husbands attending a silent retreat each year. They didn't like having their husbands gone for three days, but they were thrilled with the men who returned.

Retreat Basics

Those who plan corporate retreats can spend weeks in preparation to ensure that all the objectives are met and the time is well spent. Rest retreats, by their nature, should be more relaxed in structure and require less preparation. Because retreats should be as personal as the prayers that occur within them, I will not provide you with a detailed format, but instead offer some suggestions to get you started.

• **How long should a retreat last and how often should I go?** In my own experience, the longer the retreat, the less frequently I need to schedule them. When I take a three-day retreat, I can usually go a year before I feel the need for another one. A one-day retreat doesn't seem to hold me for more than a few months. If you've never done anything like this before and find it intimidating, you might want to test the waters with a single-day retreat. Otherwise, I would recommend a retreat no shorter than two days. It usually takes me until the second day to slow down and get into the right frame of mind to benefit from the retreat.

• **Where should I go?** If you think you would benefit from a contemplative environment, many retreat centers and monasteries offer guestrooms for those making individual retreats. If those facilities offer silent retreats or group retreats with ample time for private reflection, you may find that helpful for your first retreat or two. Otherwise, any place that takes you away from your daily routine can work as a location. For me the perfect location is one that offers miles of scenic hiking trails, as well as places to sit and reflect.

• **What should I bring with me?** For my first couple of retreats, I brought enough material to inspire me (and several of my friends) for at least a month. Sifting through the piles in order to pick out what to read became an unwanted source of stress for me. You will likely discover that reading entire books on a retreat is less restful than reflecting deeply on a particular chapter or two. In recent retreats I've taken nothing but the Bible and some notebook paper for me to jot down my thoughts and journal entries. I find the journal writing useful for crystallizing my thoughts, plus it provides a written record I can refer to after the retreat. After reviewing years of retreat journals in preparation for this chapter, I felt as if I had relived a portion of each retreat.

• **What should I expect to accomplish on this retreat?** If you are asking this question, you are approaching your retreat with the same production mentality I struggled with for years. Your work ethic is more of a hindrance than a help in this situation. I found that the harder I tried to make a perfect retreat, the less insight I received. Some writers suggest careful retreat planning, but I find that when I slow down and rest in God's presence, He directs me in the way my thinking needs to go.

So relax and don't set expectations that cause you to strive when you need to revive.

• **How should I get started on my retreat?** I almost always start my retreats by reading and reflecting on God's Word. You may want to start out by reading one of the Psalms and meditating on it (a technique described in chapter 9) for as long as you like. Later in the retreat you might want to pick a book of the Bible to work through a little bit at a time. Early in my retreat time, I take a stroll outside and praise God for all the wonderful things He has created in this world. Then I spend some time evaluating my relationship with God and let the prayer time guide me toward what areas I need to change. Please note that these activities are not the essence of the retreat, but their intent is to put you in the proper disposition for communication with God. Your job is to slow down, turn your focus to God, and allow the Holy Spirit to do the work.

• **What if I can't get past a particular situation or conflict as I start the retreat?** Sometimes, when we are facing a particularly stressful situation, we find it difficult to keep it from dominating our retreat time. I remember having a conflict with another person just before I started a one-day retreat. Throughout the day I alternated between praying to God and thinking about what I should have said to the other person to win the argument. My retreat had little impact on me until I picked up the phone and apologized for my part in the conflict.

When my wife Kathy helped lead a twenty-four-hour women's retreat, a technique they found useful was to have each woman write down all her troubles and burdens on a sheet of paper and seal it up in an envelope addressed to God. They were to put those cares in the Lord's hands for the duration of the retreat so that their focus was on God, not their problems. By the end of the retreat, many had found a sense of release from those burdens.

As you try to figure out how to wedge a retreat into your already crowded schedule, think about this: God loves you and longs to spend time alone with you. His is a standing invitation, for He is available whenever you are. As much as I love getting away with my wife or with good friends, nothing has had more of an impact on my life as those long stretches of time alone with God.

Next Step

If you keep a calendar, take a look at the next several months and select a block of days for a retreat. If your schedule is too crowded or you are still not convinced this is a priority, I'd like you to try a mini-retreat. On your next day off, commit to spending it—or at least half of it—with God. Take your Bible with you to a nearby park or other natural setting. Take a few hours to simply feel and enjoy the presence of the Lord.

Notes:

1. Emilie Griffin, *Wilderness Time: A Guide for Spiritual Retreat* (San Francisco: HarperSanFrancisco, 1997), p. 18.

2. Donald S. Whitney, *Spiritual Disciplines for the Christian Life* (Colorado Springs: NavPress, 1991), p. 177.

3. E. M. Bounds, *The Complete Works of E. M. Bounds on Prayer* (Grand Rapids, Michigan: Baker Book House, 1990), p. 460.

4. Bill Hybels, *Too Busy Not to Pray* (Downers Grove, Illinois: InterVarsity Press, 1988), p. 120.

5. Charles E. Hummel, *Freedom from Tyranny of the Urgent* (Downers Grove, Illinois: InterVarsity Press, 1997), p. 65.

Chapter 12

Keep a Constant Eye on the Fuel Gauge

Most mornings I wake up slurping coffee. When I first stumble out of bed, I wander into the kitchen to prepare my "get functional" cup of coffee, a half-filled mug I drink sitting at my desk in the study. Here I look over what the upcoming day might bring while I wait for the effects of the caffeine to take hold so I can efficiently shower and get ready for work. Throughout the workday, I always have something to drink within reach: coffee getting stale on a mug warmer in the morning and soda or herbal tea in the afternoon.

On mornings when I feel that my energy level needs more than just a shot of caffeine, I change my routine. Instead of brewing a pot of coffee for breakfast, I wipe the dust from my porcelain teapot and begin boiling water on the stove. I select one of my favorite loose teas I keep on hand, pausing to stick my nose inside the container to inhale the concentrated aromas of sweetness and spice.

Before the water reaches boiling, I pour a little from the kettle into the teapot, which warms the inside of the pot and allows the tea to remain hot a bit longer. After swirling the water around the pot until I feel the warmth on my *hands, I pour it into my teacup. This ritual helps to keep me from rushing when I drink the tea, since I would otherwise gulp my tea over letting it grow cold.*

After pouring water over the tea leaves, I thickly slice some bakery wheat bread, toast it to a pale brown, and top it with blueberry jam. At this point my tea is at the proper strength, so I pour it into the warm cup, add milk and sugar, then inhale to savor the aroma before my first sip. I hold the tea in my mouth for an extra second before swallowing, allowing all the subtle elements of its flavor to register on my tastebuds.

Instead of efficiently downing my routine dose of caffeine, the extra steps I take to brew and drink tea force me to slow down and enjoy living. Once I've spent some time soaking up one of the simple joys of life I can turn to the day's tasks with a little more vigor.

My wife and I used to differ substantially in our approach to filling our vehicles with gasoline. For Kathy, when the gauge hit the one-quarter level, she considered her vehicle out of fuel and headed right to the gas station. I, on the other hand, "knew" exactly how many miles I could drive my car without running out of gas, so I used to take it to the limit. Even the "E" symbol didn't actually mean empty to me, for even after the "idiot" light came on I knew the tank still held a final gallon or more of gasoline.

Although I never ran out of gas using this approach, it still could create a little family tension when Kathy borrowed my car or rode along with me during the last quarter tank. To her, it seemed foolish to let the fuel level get so low when it is so much easier to drive to the gas station than to walk there from your stranded vehicle, gas can in hand.

I have largely abandoned my running-on-empty method over the years, partly because of its foolishness and partly out of love for my wife. Unfortunately, my old refueling method is the approach most people take with their personal fuel gauge. "Shop 'til you drop" is a phrase that exemplifies a broader trend in a society that doesn't know when to say when. We overeat, overwork, and overexert, quitting only when we give out physically or emotionally. When people run on empty for too long, illness or burnout often result, either of which can sidetrack a person for a long time.

Being empty can be an awful thing, both to ourselves and to others who depend on us. Pastor and author Gordon MacDonald shares his own empty-tank memoirs:

> I have memories of anxieties when my father headed across the George Washington Bridge with the needle on E. But the worse memories are those times when I suddenly felt needed by someone and sensed that within me there was nothing to give. My tank was empty. There was no passion from which to operate. [1]

None of us wants to be in a situation where we need to draw upon our energy reserves, only to find out they are gone. Rather than letting our tanks run to empty, a wiser approach is to keep a watchful eye on our personal fuel level. Unfortunately, we do not come equipped with precisely marked fuel gauges, and most of us do not possess "idiot" lights to remind us that we are running out of gas.

Because we are never completely sure when "empty" will come for us, three practices will help us better ensure a proper energy level: periodic energy self-assessments, understanding the situations that drain us, and regularly scheduling activities that refuel and refresh us.

Conduct an Energy Self-Assessment

During the past couple years, I have read countless books on overwork, workaholism, stress, and burnout. The reading was informative but depressing. It is sad to consider how much of our physical and emotional woes are self-inflicted, a product of lifestyles that are out of balance and out of control. Fortunately, there are warning signs to indicate we may soon be running on fumes. I compiled the following list from some of the best books on burnout:

- You seem to be working harder and harder but accomplishing less.
- You are more irritable and short-tempered than you used to be.
- Frequently, you feel that nobody cares or nothing matters anymore.
- You are forgetting more things like appointments, deadlines, or possessions (misplacing them).

- You have more physical problems such as headaches, backaches, colds, difficulty sleeping, etc.
- Your schedule is too crowded to have time for routine errands.
- You question whether all your efforts have been worth it.
- Lately, you have become more cynical and negative.
- It is more difficult for you to make decisions.
- Increasingly, you feel helpless about finding a way out of your problems.
- You find little to be enthusiastic about and feel tired all the time.
- It is more difficult for you to concentrate or pay attention. [2]

Use these indicators as a starting point for thinking about the level of your fuel tank. Many people intuitively know where they stand, without using any assessment tools. The key is to respond to dropping energy levels before the tank reaches empty because, unlike automobiles, people can't simply pull into a filling station and be ready to roll again. Those who have experienced some level of burnout or exhaustion know that it can take months or even years to restore the zest for living again.

Be Aware of Life's Energy Drainers

Another way to guard our energy levels is to be aware of activities and situations that drain us. Knowing what wears us down can help prevent burnout because, whenever we experience such an event, we can automatically schedule more time for rest and rejuvenation.

Although many of life's energy drainers are universal, each person reacts differently to particular situations. For example, Kathy is a strong extrovert; I am an even stronger introvert. Extended time with people is a drain on me, but it tends to energize Kathy. Early in our marriage, I spent most of my workdays in meetings while Kathy spent hers at a microscope. When we had time off, she wanted to socialize, but I wanted to retreat. Once I was able to do more of my work in the home, I was able to handle our social calendar with joy instead of reluctance.

Here are a few categories of energy drainers that are more or less universal:

• **Mountaintop experiences.** When we experience something wonderful or accomplish something significant, our energy level soars to new heights—for awhile. Then, reality sets in and we come crashing down to earth. Mothers frequently experience some level of postpartum depression after giving birth. Actors feel a sense of emptiness after the curtain comes down. Writers may experience a "creative coma" shortly after the thrill of writing the final chapter of a book.

Even the great saints of God can be drained after mountaintop experiences. Elijah literally had such an experience. On Mount Carmel, God had him successfully square off against 450 prophets of Baal and 450 prophets of Asherah in a test to prove the true God of Israel. By Elijah's command, God sent fire down to consume an altar doused with water, plus brought rain to a land that had experienced a three-year drought. Shortly after being so dramatically used by God, Elijah ran off like a coward after being threatened by Jezebel, wife of King Ahab (the prophets who lost the test and their lives were hers). In 1 Kings 19:4, Elijah finds himself under a broom tree in the desert praying that he might die. "I have had enough, Lord," he said. It took forty days in the desert and an appearance of the Lord to restore him.

• **Major life changes.** Change, whether pleasant or painful, can challenge our ability to adapt and cope, causing a major energy drain. Getting married, starting a family, getting a new job, launching a business, moving to a new town/home/apartment—all of these can be exciting, but they can also take a lot out of us. Sometimes the energy loss from these situations can sneak up on us because we don't expect that something so positive can bring us to the point of exhaustion.

• **Loss or failure.** This category represents negative life changes. People we love die, close relationships might end, jobs are lost, businesses fail. A major illness, particularly one with permanent effects or chronic pain, can also fall into this category. Most of us understand that these are situations whose effects can last a long time.

• **People drains.** Many have told me that they would enjoy their work if it weren't for the people they have to deal with each day. Since we live in a world where most people are self-centered, conflict is unavoidable. Still, conflict with others can leave us hurt and expend a great deal of energy. We aggravate the situation when we seek to blame others for our problems and refuse to forgive those who harm or anger us. Another people drain can occur in one-sided relationships, where a needy person leans heavily on us for support.

• **Poor self-maintenance.** Just as an engine can break down or run sluggishly with improper fuel or maintenance, our bodies can wear down when we ignore their care. We have already discussed the effects of lack of sleep back in chapter 3. Lack of exercise also takes it toll, plus it can leave us overweight, creating both physical and emotional struggles. When we put the wrong fuel in our bodies—through poor eating habits, heavy alcohol consumption, drug use, and smoking—we will find it increasingly difficult to live life at full speed.

• **Work and scheduling drains.** For most of us, work occupies half our waking hours. For many people, it can be all-consuming. Workaholics always seem to be working. Many companies are run by workaholics who try to impose their own unhealthy schedules on their employees. Those who work two jobs to make ends meet or must work during hours the body is meant to be sleeping (those working third-shift or rotating shifts) will constantly fight fatigue. Caregivers—both health-care professionals and those caring for sick family members—face emotional strain in addition to the physical demands of the work. Work that is meaningless or unsatisfying to the one performing it is like walking through life dragging a ball and chain—ask anyone who has escaped to an enjoyable work calling. Constant deadline pressure, whether it is a product of a poorly managed employer or our own schedule overloading, can burn out a person in short order. Simply put, trying to do too much is exhausting.

• **Brain drains.** Sometimes it is what goes on inside our heads that drains us. How we feel about what we are experiencing is often more important than the event itself. Fear, anxiety, guilt, frustration, denial, and depression can cause us to not even want to get out of bed in the morning. According to Dr. Paul Reisser, M.D., in his book *Energy Drainers, Energy Gainers,* our emotional state can dramatically affect our outlook on life, especially our "expectations for the immediate future." Expectations that are unrealistic or otherwise unmet can be crushing, particularly when they deal with more critical areas of our lives. [3]

Discover and Do What Refreshes You

With all these potential energy drainers out there, it is critical that we develop our own personal list of energy "refuelers." These refuelers can be both activities that offset the effects of life's stresses and those that directly raise our energy levels. This list may vary more from person to person than the list of what drains us. Still, I see several practices that seem to recharge most people:

• **Sleep.** Eight to ten hours of quality sleep each night will do wonders for fatigue. If you can't stay asleep for that long a stretch, try taking naps in the afternoon. (Many of the world's greatest thinkers, including Albert Einstein and Winston Churchill, were frequent nappers.)

• **Rest and simple relaxation.** You would certainly expect to find the old "R and R" prescription in a book on rest. But simple relaxation can offset the draining effects of stress. According to Dr. Archibald Hart, if each challenge is followed by a "state of calmness," and each day and week ends with rest, then "you will be healthy in body, mind, and spirit—and all of your stress will be 'good.'" [4]

• **Prayer.** As we've seen earlier, prayer can have a quieting, restful impact on us. It also allows us to further develop our relationship with God, which Dr. Reisser calls "the ultimate energy gainer, because God is the ultimate source of all purpose and power." [5]

• **Regular, aerobic exercise.** When we exercise regularly in a way that increases our heart rate without overdoing it, it reduces our stress and gives us more energy for daily living. Dr. Reisser calls exercise "one of the few activities that increase energy. I rarely see a chronically tired person who is exercising regularly and reasonably." [6]

• **Enjoyment of life's simple pleasures.** We can turn a golden sunset or holding hands with a loved one into "minivacations" of sorts. A relaxing hobby or playing with a child can recharge us for when we return to our work and other obligations.

Once we have a feel for what our energy burners and refuelers are, we can keep a safe fuel level by learning to alternate these items on our schedules. For example, during a speaking engagement on the other side of the country, I experienced four items on my energy-burner list: travel in unfamiliar areas, a tight work deadline, extended time with people, and the speaking engagement itself. To make matters worse, airplane mechanical problems forced me to stay overnight in a strange city, plus my suitcase made it home six hours later than I did. The unexpected extra travel day was the day I had scheduled for rest, so I was not in top shape as I drove home from the airport. Since I had no suitcase to unpack, I decided to take a detour to the beach. My spirits picked up considerably as I strolled along one of New England's most beautiful beaches, thanking God for the weekend and for bringing me home safely.

Next Step

Take a few minutes pondering what your fuel gauge would read right now if you had one. Would it read full, half-full, quarter-full, or empty? Spend some time jotting down a list of energy burners and refuelers. This next week, add at least one item from your refueler list to your schedule.

Notes:

1. Gordon MacDonald, *Restoring Your Spiritual Passion* (Nashville: Thomas

Nelson Publishers, 1986), p. 57.

2. Primary sources for this list are: Dr. Herbert J. Freudenberger, *Burn-Out: The High Cost of High Achievement* (New York: Anchor Press/Doubleday, 1980), pp. 17-18; Frank Minirth, Paul Meier, Don Hawkins, Chris Thurman, and Richard Flournoy, *Beating Burnout* (New York: Inspirational Press, 1997), pp. 37-38.

3. Dr. Paul Reisser, M.D., *Energy Drainers, Energy Gainers* (Grand Rapids, Michigan: Zondervan Publishing House, 1990), p. 25.

4. Dr. Archibald D. Hart, *The Hidden Link Between Adrenalin and Stress* (Dallas: Word Publishing, 1991), p. 34.

5. Reisser, p. 159.

6. Ibid., p. 81.

Part IV:
Creating More Rest
in the World Around Us

So far we have looked at a variety of ways to find more rest in our lives. These practices are easy to implement—should you happen to live alone on a tropical island. Most of us, however, live, work, and worship in the middle of a restless culture filled with restless people. To be successful in our quest for rest, we need to learn how to overcome the obstacles to rest that may be present in our relationships with others, in our homes and communities, and in the values of our culture.

The chapters in this section will not only help you maintain rest in a restless culture, but will provide some ideas on how to better create environments—where you live, work, study, or worship—that are more conducive to rest for everyone involved.

Chapter 13

Learning to Forgive and Forget

B rian woke up before the music began playing on his clock radio. As the early morning sunshine began to filter through the curtains, he watched his wife sleeping beside him. He couldn't believe that last night she complained again about his long hours at work. She didn't seem to mind when he received his promotion last year, and she certainly had been quick to spend the extra money as fast as it came in. Of course, if he spent more time at home, she would just have more opportunities to nag him about other things. So what was the point?

He rose from bed and wandered down the hall to a locked bathroom door. That would be Heather, using up all the hot water with one of her endless showers. Now that she was in college, she acted as if she were too smart for her father. Just last week, when he tried to join in a discussion on one of her classes, she interrupted him, saying, "What could a corporate slave possibly know about philosophy?"

As he trudged off toward the kitchen, he muttered something about seeing how well his daughter could pay for her overpriced education if he stopped footing the bills for awhile. He was grateful that he programmed the coffee *pot to brew at an earlier time this week, so at least there was something around here he wouldn't have to wait for.*

He backed his sedan out of the garage and noticed Mitch leaving for work at the same time. Mitch tried a half-wave of his hand, but Brian did his best to ignore his neighbor. He refused to speak to Mitch and Connie ever since their dog bit Heather when she was small. They had the nerve to suggest that his daughter might have been mostly to blame for getting bit.

After dealing with the usual "jerks" on the highway, Brian was glad to arrive at work with some time to spare before his first meeting. Within minutes of easing into his leather chair, his boss Ron appeared in the doorway with another last-minute project. Brian dutifully accepted the work without saying a word. Ever since Ron took the credit for one of Brian's best ideas last quarter, the relationship had been strained. One of these days Ron would make a mistake and Brian would nail him to the wall and finally have the position he deserved.

The world is filled with bitter people—people with so much anger built up inside that they would make Brian look like Pollyanna by comparison.

Unfortunately, we humans are selfish creatures with egos far larger than we might let on. With billions of prideful people inhabiting the earth, hostility and conflict are inevitable. Sometimes our feelings get a little bruised. Other times the pain is more substantial.

Over the course of a lifetime, most of us will accumulate enough hurts to drain our hearts dry, leaving us angry, bitter, and empty, with little left to offer others. These accumulated hurts can also rob us of rest. The doctors of the Minirth-Meier Clinic call bitterness, which is the result of holding grudges, "the most significant factor in burnout." They see more patients burning out from bitterness than from either stress or perfectionism. [1]

Letting It Out vs. Letting It Go

The world's wisdom regarding anger and hurt differs radically from the wisdom found in the Bible. Our culture takes a self-centered approach to conflict. We are supposed to stand up for our rights. If we get angry, we are not to hold it in; rather we need to express it, to let it out. In fact, some "experts" claim that conflict in relationships can be a healthy thing. The world's ultimate answer to getting hurt is to seek justice and/or a punitive monetary settlement.

The Bible, on the other hand, sees human conflict as dangerous and sinful. Proverbs 17:14 states, "Starting a quarrel is like breaching a dam; so drop the matter before a dispute breaks out." Conflict is indeed like a flood, for once it starts it is difficult to contain. And for those who love a good fight, they "love sin" according to Proverbs 17:19.

One of our obligations as Christians, according to Hebrews 12:14 and other passages, is to "make every effort to live in peace with all men." Sometimes, despite our best efforts, conflicts still arise. Yet I have found that disputes can rarely be sustained without participation from more than one side. In reflecting on my own problems with others over the years, I almost always find my pride to be a major contributing factor. Someone hurt my feelings or punctured my ego. Someone didn't agree with my brilliant idea. Someone made me do something I didn't want to do.

When I agree with Proverbs 13:10 that "pride only breeds quarrels," it is a little easier to deal with the anger. Even if I believe that I am "right" in terms of the dispute, I am wrong to let my pride cause problems with others—and I have a sin that I need to confess to God and to the other party. This approach has not made my life conflict-free, but it does eliminate most of them or at least ensures they don't last long.

According to Scripture, we are not to have any long-lasting disputes. Instead, we are instructed in Ephesians 4:26 to "not let the sun go down while [we] are still angry." God knows that when we let our anger stew, it grows immensely. Our imagination and emotions feed on each other until the conflict seems like World War II, and we have so vilified our opponent that he or she seems like Hitler to us.

The Bible instructs us to go at once to the source of our conflict or hurt to settle it, so it does not fester and grow. If we have some blame in the matter, Jesus tells us in Matthew 5:24 to "go and be reconciled to your brother." What if we are the victim? In Matthew 18:15-17, Jesus offers sound advice, particularly regarding situations with other Christians:

If your brother sins against you, go and show him his fault, just between the two of you. If he listens to you, you have won your brother over. But if he will not listen, take one or two others along, so that "every matter may be established by the testimony of two or three witnesses." If he refuses to listen to them, tell it to the church; and if he refuses to listen even to the church, treat him as you would a pagan or a tax collector.

I have seen relationships shattered and churches split in two because this practice of reconciliation was not followed. It is so much easier to vent our pain and anger to others than to go to its source. Unfortunately, telling others does nothing to make us the peacemakers that God blesses; it only makes us gossips.

Now let's turn to a tougher issue. Do we forgive the repeat offender? In the world's view, we might be willing to forgive a person once, giving her a second chance. If she blows her chance, she had better not even think about crawling back for our forgiveness.

In Matthew 18:21-22, Peter asked Jesus how many times he was to forgive someone who sinned against him. "Up to seven times?" he asked, thinking himself magnanimous. Jesus' response must have floored him. "I tell you, not seven times, but seventy-seven times."

Jesus follows this statement by telling the Parable of the Unmerciful Servant, which provides the Bible's best answer to the question: Why should I forgive others? A servant was brought before his master to settle his debts. The man owed the equivalent of millions of dollars and lacked the means to pay, so the master ordered that the servant, his family, and all he owed be sold to pay the debt. The servant fell on his knees and begged for mercy, promising to repay the debt. At this the master took pity on him, canceled the debt, and let him go. What did the "grateful" servant do? He found a fellow servant who owed him a tiny sum of money and demanded repayment. When the man begged for mercy, the servant threw him into prison until he could pay his debt. Of course, when the master found out, he was angry with the servant for refusing to show even a fraction of the mercy he had just received, and then threw the unforgiving servant in jail. Jesus concluded the parable with these words: "This is how my heavenly Father will treat each of you unless you forgive your brother from your heart" (Matthew 18:35).

This message is a real eye-opener when we let it sink in. If we refuse to forgive others, God will not forgive our sins. When you think about the mountain of sins God is willing to forgive throughout our lives because of our relationship with Jesus, for us to withhold forgiveness from another person is a slap in the face to God. We can't possibly appreciate the mercy He has shown us if we are unwilling to offer even the tiniest dose of it to others.

If we look at the Lord's Prayer found in Matthew 6 and Luke 11, we find only one part of the prayer that is conditional: God will forgive us our debts or trespasses "as we forgive" our debtors or those who trespass against us. Just in case we missed the point, Jesus followed up the prayer with this statement in Matthew 6:14-15: "For if you forgive men when they sin against you, your heavenly Father will also forgive you. But if you do not forgive men their sins, your Father will not forgive your sins."

As Christians, forgiving others is not optional—that is, unless we don't mind coming to the throne of God to be judged for our own sins. John Wesley, the founder of Methodism, adeptly explained how God forgives us as we forgive others:

If any malice or bitterness and if any taint of unkindness or anger remains, if we do not clearly, fully and from the heart forgive all others their trespasses, we so far cut short the forgiveness of our own trespasses. God cannot clearly and fully forgive us; he may show us some degree of mercy, but we will not suffer him to blot out all our sins and forgive all our iniquities. [2]

If we want God to forgive our wickedness and remember our sins no more (Jeremiah 31:34), we need to do the same.

Another good reason for forgiving others is the benefit we receive from doing so. When we hold a grudge, we think we are punishing the other person when, in fact, we are the ones being hurt. The people who hurt us are not losing sleep over what they have done to us. We are the ones who are prisoners to the anger and rage that drain us. When we forgive, we can taste freedom again.

Freedom is exactly how Walter Everett describes his forgiveness of the man who murdered his adult son. One year after his son was murdered, this pastor wrote a letter to the killer in prison. He told the man about the anger he had felt, but added with great difficulty that he forgave him. That night his son's murderer knelt beside his prison bunk and prayed to receive the forgiveness of Jesus Christ. The two men began to write to one another and Walter began making prison visits. Years later, he was minister at the man's wedding. Although he initially wondered if forgiveness was possible in this case, he notes that God freed him "from the stranglehold of anger and resentment." [3]

Can the Wrongs Ever Be Forgotten?

I debated for quite awhile about whether to include the word *forget* in the chapter title. When I first taught on forgiveness, I had some resistance from the class on the concept of forgetting. I couldn't even find agreement among the various research sources I consulted. Some say forgetting is possible; a few doubt that it is even desirable.

I must admit to seeing some validity in these objections, especially concerning life's major hurts. Someone who is raped or has an unfaithful or abusive spouse is unlikely to forget the experience. I doubt that Walter Everett will ever erase the memory of his son's murder.

Still, I think an important part of gaining the freedom and the rest benefits of forgiveness is to stop "actively remembering" the wrong. It is natural to replay a situation or an argument over and over again in our heads. We all do this. I am particularly adept at thinking up clever arguments or one-liners I wish I had thought to say at the time or would like to say next time I see the person.

This replaying of the incident, plus the rehearsal of our "comeback" lines, does little more than keep the pain fresh in our minds. True forgiveness involves taking the other person off the hook, both in reality and in our imaginations. Nineteenth-century clergyman Henry Ward Beecher once noted, "'I can forgive, but I cannot forget,' is only another way of saying 'I cannot forgive.'" Sydney Harris puts it more colorfully: "There's no point in burying a hatchet if you're going to put up a marker on the site." [4]

Within 1 Corinthians 13 is found one of the most beautiful descriptions of love ever written. In verse five, right after the part about love not being easily angered, comes the statement that love "keeps no record of wrongs." The Greek word translated as "no record" is often translated as *count* or *credited*. When we look at a person and find we can create every unkind word, have memorized every slight we may have received from him, we are not demonstrating love. We are especially not showing love if we continue to bring up those past wrongs in everyday conversations, as people in unhealthy marriages often do.

In reality, this issue of forgiving and forgetting is an effective indicator of who is on the throne of our hearts: Jesus or self. When Jesus is our Lord, our focus is on God and His mercy, His many blessings, and the love we experience in others. When we retain our "kingdom," our focus is on ourselves, on how we've been hurt or shortchanged, on how others have disappointed us. According to Phillip Keller, "We are often quick to forget our blessings, slow to forget our misfortunes." [5]

As we grow in our relationship with Jesus, the Holy Spirit inside us transforms us over time, so we become less self-absorbed and more grateful. It is that transformation that increasingly makes forgiveness and even forgetting possible.

Next Step

Do you have a relationship in which there is an unresolved hurt or conflict? Whether you are the one who needs to forgive or to ask forgiveness, make a point to contact that person as soon as you are able. Pray to God for guidance in how to handle the situation. If the problem is current, it is probably best to be handled in person, while sins of the distant past may be able to be addressed in writing. In the case of major issues, such as rape, abuse, or adultery, I would strongly suggest you consult with a pastor or pastoral counselor before initiating any personal contact. These situations usually require far more than a simple "I'm sorry" and "you're forgiven" to bring about any resolution.

Also, spend a few minutes reflecting on one of your close relationships, perhaps your spouse or a close friend. Make a list of all the things you like or love about the person, all the good times you have shared together. This exercise helps us to keep a record of "rights" to counter and eventually take the place of our record of "wrongs." The next time you are alone with that person, share one of the items from your list.

Notes:

1. Frank Minirth, Paul Meier, Don Hawkins, Chris Thurman, and Richard Flournoy, *Beating Burnout* (New York: Inspirational Press, 1997), p. 226.
2. John Wesley, "Forgiving from Our Hearts," *Decision*, December 1996, p. 34.
3. Walter H. Everett, "Forgiving the Man Who Killed My Son," *Decision*, December 1996, p. 32.
4. Tony Castle, *The New Book of Christian Quotations* (New York: Crossroad Publishing Company, 1988), p. 89.
5. Phillip Keller, *A Shepherd Looks at Psalm 23* (Grand Rapids, Michigan: Zondervan Publishing House, 1970), p. 79.

Chapter 14

Creating Rest Where You Live, Work, and Worship

It was Thursday morning, and the four members of the Collins family gathered together for breakfast as they nearly always did. Hank and Linda sipped their coffee while Melissa and Michael told their parents of the upcoming day at school.

"Sounds like marching band practice has been going well, Melissa. Your father and I are looking forward to seeing you march in the parade next weekend."

"Michael, is it our turn to drive you and the guys to soccer practice on Saturday?"

"No, Dad. Chad's parents are taking us this weekend. Your turn doesn't come around again for two more weeks. When are you and Mom going to be back from the church reflection cottage?"

"We're spending all day Friday and Saturday at the cottage, so we'll be back Saturday evening. Your grandparents are coming over to stay with you two."

"How come you have Friday off, Dad?"

"Well, we finished that big project we've been working so hard on, and it helped us land a significant new client. Our president was so pleased that she's serving pizza to the whole company for lunch, plus everyone gets Friday off with pay. As soon as I heard that, your mother and I booked the church cottage so we can enjoy some extra time with each other and with God."

"Is the reflection cottage nice?"

"Oh, it's nothing fancy, much like the place you kids go for retreats. But it's located on a beautiful lake, and it is so quiet! This summer we'll schedule the place for a few days so we can have a family retreat."

"Before I forget," Linda interjected, "what do you kids want to do for family night? Since your father and I are going away for a couple days, I thought it would be great to spend an extra evening this week doing something special together."

After much spirited discussion, the Collins family reached consensus on spending the evening splashing around at the municipal swimming pool.

Does this family situation sound a little too perfect? The Black family seems out of step with life in the twenty-first century. They eat meals together, they talk, they don't act rushed, and they have time to spend together. Their home, work, and church environments all appear to help them stay rested, instead of wearing them down. It sounds great—except things don't usually work that way in the real world.

The home should be a refuge from the wearying pace of the world. Instead, we too often have a house filled with busy strangers who stop by to eat, sleep, bicker with one another, and watch television. The workplace can be an exciting outlet for our talents and interests. Instead, it tends to be a never-ending source of meaninglessness, conflict, and stress. The church, of all places, should provide an environment where we can quiet our souls and rekindle our relationship with God. Instead, the "house of God" is typically filled with as much meaningless activity and conflict as the workplace, run by pastors and other leaders who are on a pace to burn out or drop out in just a few short years.

Although each of us is influenced by the restlessness of our environments, we also can play a role in changing them for the better. Trying to alter the conditions around us is valuable for two reasons. First, it is one way for us to love our neighbor. Galatians 6:2 instructs us, "Carry each other's burdens, and in this way you will fulfill the law of Christ."

Second, creating a more restful environment for others will make our own rest easier. Proverbs 11:25 states that "he who refreshes others will himself be refreshed."

For example, keeping a Sabbath day of rest works best when it is a family affair. I initially tried resting on Sundays alone, without attempting to convince my wife to join me. Those first days were almost comical, with one of us a blur of activity and the other a "bum." At least that is how I felt. With Kathy working so hard around the house, it was hard to sit still without feeling guilty. The guilt took away much of the rest value of the day. Only when Kathy and I both decided to slow down on Sundays did my Sabbaths become more restful.

How do we create more rest in our homes, workplaces, and churches? The next pages will provide some suggestions. For each arena, we will explore how the institution can better ensure the rest of those within it, plus how we can help bring those changes about. Although we all may be able to bring about some changes at the family level, it may require more creativity to make changes at work or church, particularly if we do not serve in a position of leadership. But real change can occur regardless of where we happen to be situated on the organizational chart.

Help for the Hurried Home

"Help for the Hurried Home" is the subtitle of the book *Little House on the Freeway*, written by Tim Kimmel. Look at some of the marks of a hurried household, according to Kimmel: too busy to relax, can't enjoy quiet, never feel satisfied, live with shifting situational standards, overworked and under-appreciated, worry about things we can't control, and are not happy unless we are successful.[1]

Do any of those attributes describe your household, your family? Unfortunately, if you answered yes for a number of those traits, you are hardly alone. Most households are hurried these days; many would more aptly be described as frantic.

What can be done to "unhurry" our homes? Since any solutions will involve multiple people, easing the clutter of a household's schedule will take a concerted effort and some small sacrifices from everyone involved. Here are a few suggestions, for starters:

• **Limit each family member to one individual outside-the-home pursuit at a time.** In hyperactive households, children and parents can be involved in so many activities outside of the home that there are no times slots left for the whole family to be together. Put one child in two different sports at a time, plus music or dance lessons, and you have a busy child—and probably a busy parent trying to get the child to all his or her activities. Multiply this by several children and you have scheduling madness on your hands.

If your household resembles Grand Central Station, it is important to regain some control for your children's sake as well as for your own. People think they are doing their children a great service by allowing them so many opportunities for activity and learning. Yet, many experts now say our children are far too overscheduled. Although learning opportunities are important, children also require large chunks of time for play and simply being with their parents.

During the next year, try to limit each family member (yourself included) to one major activity outside the home at a time. For example, bowling and playing on a softball team might both be allowed because bowling leagues often take the summer off. A golf league and softball (or playing on more than one softball team) would not work because it bunches together two outside commitments during the summer season.

This suggestion may sound drastic to some fast-track families. You may also encounter significant resistance from one or more family members. (It will help somewhat if you allow each person to choose the activity he or she wishes to keep.) If you are skeptical, I still encourage you to try this for a year. After that, I doubt you will ever want to go back to the way it used to be.

• **Identify pursuits to enjoy as a couple or family.** This step should help alleviate concerns some might have about giving up any of their individual pursuits. Activities that can be done as a couple or family not only meet our recreational needs, but help build closer relationships.

One approach I have found useful comes from psychologist Willard F. Harley Jr. in his book *His Needs, Her Needs: Building an Affair-proof Marriage.* He advises couples to each make a list of all the activities he or she enjoys doing—at least forty to fifty items each. Then he has them compile their lists and have both husband and wife rate each activity from a +4 (absolutely love) to a -4 (absolutely hate). When Kathy and I did this, we identified more than a dozen activities we both enjoyed doing—and most of them we were not doing at the time. I set a goal each year for us to pursue one new activity together. Sometimes the activity ends up becoming a major pastime like sailing. Often it is a short-term or fun pursuit like taking tap-dancing lessons together (that one, believe it or not, was my idea). The net result is a closer relationship with a growing number of common interests.

Harley believes that couples who play together stay together. He also cites a rule he makes for couples who come to him for counseling—a rule I thought too strict at first. "If any recreational activity enjoyed by one spouse bothers the other spouse or cannot include the other spouse, it must be abandoned." [2]

Regardless of your reaction to the last statement, it might be useful to try to compile an activity list as a couple and/or as a family. Even the most diverse family should be able to come up with a few areas of common interest. Imagine the logistics for a family of four when one person goes to a movie, one plays tennis, another goes hiking, while still another heads out on in-line skates. If everyone in the family enjoys swimming, for example, think about how much easier it would be for all four to spend some time together at the community pool.

• **Pick one family relationship to work on building or repairing.** In the last chapter we saw how relationship conflicts can create an imposing obstacle to rest. According to Dr. Richard Swenson, fractured relationships are "perhaps the greatest root cause for the absence of rest in our society." [3]

You may or may not have any fractured relationships to deal with, but most hurried households have at least one relationship that has suffered some neglect. Pick one relationship to work on during the next year. If your marriage is not as strong as it should be, make that the relationship you work on, even if you have problems with children as well, because a close husband-wife bond provides a solid foundation for parent-child relationships.

Commit to setting aside a significant amount of time each week for that person, especially time for just the two of you. If you do something together, pick activities you know the other person especially enjoys rather than your own favorites. If you have had disagreements in the past, apologize for your role in the conflict and tell the other person that you love him or her and want to do a better job in the relationship. Over time, most family relationships can be considerably strengthened if given proper attention and time.

• **Practice carrying each other's burdens.** This suggestion is simply living out the command found in Galatians 6:2. If mutual helpfulness is not a common practice in your household, you may need to take some initiative to get the ball rolling. For starters, identify the most stressed-out or overloaded member of your household (yourself excluded). Then identify one area of household or personal chores that you can volunteer to take over for the next several weeks. If you do this on a regular basis, you should eventually find others in the family willing to help out when you are under heavy stress.

When Kathy attended graduate school, I took on additional household duties, including a much larger share of the cooking. Just after she graduated, I received a contract to write my first book and the roles were reversed. Having someone to pitch in during our busy cycles sure keeps the stress under control. (By the way, if you are married to a compulsive workaholic, pitching in will only enable him or her to take on still more work—get help with his or her problem instead.)

• **Schedule sit-down, TV-free meals.** For many centuries, meals have been the main time for the family to gather and discuss matters both important and trivial. Now most families—if their schedules permit them to eat together at all—feed their faces while staring blankly at the television screen. If you are one of those families, consider scheduling at least one meal a week that is served at the table without a television present. The first few times you try this, expect a lot of awkward moments of silence until people rediscover the lost art of conversation.

For nearly all of my life I have eaten my evening meals with television instead of conversation. In fact, one of our most-used household items was the TV lap-tray with beanbag bottom I balanced on the arm of our sofa while munching in front of the television. During the past year Kathy has begun serving meals regularly at the dining room table, and we've discovered that our mealtime talks are much more interesting than anything we could click to with our remote control. The new routine has also helped us avoid watching more television after dinner, freeing up time for more creative and enjoyable pursuits.

Building a Saner Workplace

For many people, work is a major contributor to their lack of rest. Ever since the fall of Adam, work has been difficult. However, as our culture becomes more restless, it has given birth to legions of restless organizations. You find these organizations in every field in the world of work, particularly in those high-technology areas that are supposed to create much of the new employment during the twenty-first century.

Restless organizations move at a frantic pace. They seem to be in a constant crisis mode, dealing with market changes or internal challenges. Those with salaried positions are pressured—both directly and indirectly—to work hours resembling those in the sweatshops of the Industrial Age. Restless organizations are constantly changing strategies, moving from project to project with little thought as to the big picture. As a result, a ton of work-related activity occurs, but little of any enduring value is accomplished. The other constantly changing feature of a restless work site is the people. Overloaded employees either burn out and leave, or simply leave for greener or saner pastures.

Those working in restless organizations can take heart. Not every organization drains the last ounce of life from its employees. New, kinder workplaces are emerging that recognize the integrity and worth of their employees. Some employers are learning a secret that should be obvious: create an environment where people can thrive and you can build an organization that accomplishes great things.

The following suggestions may help managers and business owners create a saner work environment, plus provide other workers with an idea of what to look for when seeking a less stressful employment situation.

• **Encourage and enforce reasonable work hours.** Over the long haul, neither employer nor employee benefits from regularly working sixty- to eighty-hour weeks. Rather than letting their employees work themselves to exhaustion, some employers believe excessively long workweeks are a sign that something is wrong with the way the company or the employee is doing the job. One employer told me that if he was working eighty-hour weeks, he was denying another person the opportunity to work, learn, and earn. In his company, employees are limited to four weeks a year when their work hours may exceed fifty hours, which allows for emergencies and other deadlines that pop up. If the job cannot be done in those time limits, its demands and the performance of the employee will be reviewed.

Other employers find different ways to create limits on time spent working. One company locks its gates at 6 P.M. every night to better ensure its employees go home and spend time with their families. Another locks its gates on Sunday to enforce at least one day of rest for all of its employees. Chick-fil-A closes all its fast-food chicken restaurants on Sundays in obedience to God's Sabbath commandment, a remarkable achievement given that the day is traditionally one of the industry's busiest in terms of sales.

• **Offer employees more flexibility in when and where they work.** More and more employers are offering greater flexibility in terms of what hours employees do their work. Some are allowing employees to perform part, most, or all of their duties while working from home. One area where employers need to improve is in providing part-time options for more highly skilled workers. Most part-time jobs are currently entry-level positions, offering low pay, no benefits, and little chance for advancement. Good-paying part-time positions could provide many people with meaningful work, as well as more time to spend with family and other pursuits. Also, employers who offer these kinds of jobs usually attract a flood of highly motivated and loyal workers.

Creating a part-time position for myself was a critical step in making the transition from a marketing executive in the health care field to a writer/teacher/entrepreneur. As I was approaching the six-year mark with HealthEast, I had other career goals and was ready for a change.

By allowing me to create a three-day-a-week position in my department, my boss was able to double my length of stay at the company. Without the reduced hours, I don't know how or if my career transition would have taken place.

• **Make jobs more meaningful.** When employees see no meaning or hope in their work, they lack motivation and can easily burn out. Often, employers create more motivated workers simply by taking the time to explain how their work fits into the big picture, how their work is important to meeting company goals. Ensuring that employees find work tasks best suited to their abilities and interests is another simple concept that pays big dividends in terms of energizing workers. Also, simple praise and recognition for good work helps employees feel appreciated and makes all their hard work seem worthwhile.

• **Provide celebrations and time off after a major push at work.** Periodically, every organization has major projects or challenges that require people to work harder and longer to see it through. When the project ends, most companies just hurry their people off to do all the work that has been piling up in other areas. Smart employers know that people need a break. The kind of celebration and time off mentioned in the chapter opening does wonders for recharging the energy levels of weary workers. It recognizes their hard work and tells them their employer cares about them, not just the job they do.

• **Create a team atmosphere where people help each other out.** In most organizations, boundaries are high between departments and other work units. "It's not my job" becomes the answer to any request to help out another overworked employee or department. Some employers, however, have managed to create a system where boundaries are few and people work together as a team. For this to work, top management needs to model the team approach, even to the point of being willing to help out in the trenches when workloads dictate. Also, management needs to create incentives, financial and otherwise, that compensate employees based on the organization's success. When everyone pitches in to help, workplace stress and burnout is significantly reduced.

Restoring Rest in Churches

Churches could and should be an important rest resource in our communities. Too often our churches are just another place of endless activity and conflict. We seem to offer more church-related programs than ever before, but are they creating more spiritually mature believers or winning more souls to Christ? This flurry of religious activity can sometimes lead to burnout, both for pastors and church members. Let's take a look at their stresses separately.

Pastors have one of the most stressful jobs around. One survey of pastors indicated that 70 percent of them work more than sixty hours a week and 85 percent spend two or fewer nights at home per week. [4]

Several factors contribute to this workload and the resulting high rate of burnout. The first factor I call the "Superhero Syndrome." Most pastors are in situations with an almost unlimited number of hurting people and other ministry needs. The problem is they think they need to meet all those needs. Jesus didn't heal all the sick in Israel or preach in every town, but for some reason pastors often refuse to accept such limits for themselves. Pastors who can't rest until all the work is done will never rest.

"It's the pastor's job" is another factor in clergy burnout. Particularly in small churches, everything remotely connected with church is considered the pastor's job. In the New Testament, all believers were to participate in church ministry—there were no "laypeople" back then.

"They work only on Sundays" is the final factor contributing to ministry stress. Unknowing pew-sitters see the pastor working only on Sundays, so they assume the job isn't too demanding. As a result, some churches are unsympathetic to pastors who want time off, or want to spend more time reading, studying, and praying. We need to be careful not to overload our pastors or try to make them guilty for wanting to take some time off. We also need to cultivate more spiritual leaders in the church who can better shoulder some of the pastor's workload.

Pastors are not alone in their struggles. For example, "missionary furlough" has become an oxymoron. It is supposed to be a leave of absence from the rigors of the mission field, a time to rest and visit with friends and family. I recall receiving a letter from some friends on the mission field describing the activities on their upcoming three-month furlough. It was a relentless schedule of presentations to update churches on their progress and seek out new financial supporters to replace those who had fallen by the wayside. They even felt the need to stress to their prayer partners that they weren't going to be spending their furlough resting. Does this sound like the proper way to rejuvenate missionaries for their next stint of duty?

Pastors and missionaries aren't the only ones who can burn out serving God. It is important that pastors and other church leaders be sympathetic to the needs of their members. The members of their "flock" have lives that are a lot busier than before, meaning they need to be more selective in what they get involved with. Pastors need to be careful not to add to the burden by making members feel guilty if they don't attend every church meeting or get involved in every worthwhile program. If people aren't showing up for something, don't put all the blame on them. Perhaps something is wrong with what is being offered, or it may be held on a day and time that is inconvenient for many people. For example, in an age when most women work outside the home, the majority of churches still hold their women's Bible studies on weekdays during normal working hours.

According to Robert Banks, author of *The Tyranny of Time*, many church programs, committees, organizations, and even buildings should be temporary in nature, serving a needed purpose, then coming to an end. He adds, "All Christian activities should come up for periodic review and be required to justify their continued existence." [5]

All organizations, churches included, need to understand that if you keep adding new activities without eliminating any existing ones, two things are likely to occur. One, people doing the activities will eventually burn out, and few or none of the projects will be done effectively. Two, a crammed-full church schedule doesn't allow room for God to tell the church what He wants to do through them. Churches that are too busy don't have time to pray for God's leading, much less act on what He asks. Since we live in communities with far more ministry needs than resources, doesn't it make sense to pray and wait for God's leading instead of wearing ourselves out trying to do more than God would want us to attempt?

Finally, churches could become more of a beacon of rest and light by providing people with opportunities for quiet stillness before God.

Church services and even prayer meetings often seem rushed and noisy. When was the last time in church that we stopped the music and our collective yapping long enough to spend some substantial time in quiet prayer? Do church retreats set aside more than a few minutes for quiet prayer or are we rushing to pack as much activity into the days as possible? Another way to help create rest would be to build small meditation rooms or chapels in quiet parts of church buildings where individuals could come to escape the world's noise and be with God. We could also do a better job of teaching people how to pray.

As Christians we need to better encourage one another in our efforts to find more rest because we aren't going to find much help elsewhere in the world. Just as weary travelers are grateful for the sight of a rest area on a long stretch of highway, many will benefit from any oasis of rest that we help create in our homes, workplaces, and churches.

Next Step

Do you reside in a hurried home? Schedule an evening meeting with everyone in the household to discuss ways to bring more sanity to your home. First, discuss some of the reasons for your family's busyness, as well as the problems the hectic pace creates. Then let each person share ideas to help ease the strain. You may want to share a couple of suggestions from this chapter to get the ideas flowing. Then, have the family vote on which idea or ideas to try during the next month.

Notes:

1. Tim Kimmel, *Little House on the Freeway* (Portland, Oregon: Multnomah Press, 1987), p. 18-25.
2. Willard F. Harley Jr., *His Needs, Her Needs: Building an Affair-proof Marriage* (Old Tappen, New Jersey: Fleming H. Revell Company, 1986), p. 81.
3. Richard A. Swenson, M.D., *Margin* (Colorado Springs: NavPress, 1992), p. 232.

4. Frank Minirth, Paul Meier, Don Hawkins, Chris Thurman, and Richard Flournoy, *Beating Burnout* (New York: Inspirational Press, 1997), p. 83.
5. Robert Banks, *The Tyranny of Time* (Downers Grove, Illinois: InterVarsity Press, 1983), p. 247.

Chapter 15

Step Back from the Material World

J anet removed the stack of envelopes from her top desk drawer and reached for the family checkbook. Every month the pile of bills and their balances seemed to grow, while the balance of the checkbook continued to shrink. This was a task she had been putting off all week, but she couldn't wait any longer without incurring late fees on top of the interest owed.

As she opened the first credit card bill, Janet let out a groan. Spending each Saturday at the mall last month, she knew her balance would soar a bit, but this last trip put her close to her credit limit. *Better call and see if the limit can be raised again,* she thought. *Last year the card company doubled it without even asking any questions.* Since this card's balance dwarfed what was in her checking account, paying it off was hardly an option. Janet wrote out a check for the minimum monthly payment.

The next credit card was the one Tom primarily used, mainly for business travel, automotive expenses, and his recreational "toys." The toy category accounted for most of the balance, particularly since last year's promotion at work allowed him to buy the high-speed motorboat he had always wanted. The fact that the boat touched the water just once all year didn't lower the cost of outfitting the boat of his dreams. It could join the growing collection of shiny objects with motors gathering dust in the garage. Now he had his eye on some lake property north of town. Just as long as he doesn't charge the purchase to this card, she thought. Another check was written for the minimum payment.

Next came the department store charge card, with its balance still swollen from last year's back-to-school shopping for the children. Janet had planned to pay off the balance before another year of school expenses arrived. With a new school year just around the corner, that goal would not be realized. Janet made a mental note to put this year's shopping on one of the bank credit cards to avoid exceeding her limit on the store card.

The next credit card envelope contained the financial damage from last month's vacation. Being on vacation, she and Tom tried not to worry about what things cost when they were supposed to be relaxing. A week of eating out, shopping, and inflated tourist prices gave Janet plenty to worry about when the bill arrived. She made out a check to cover the minimum payment once again.

After writing checks for the mortgage, home equity loan, and lease payments for both vehicles, Janet concluded by calculating the final balance in her account to see how much she'd have left over for grocery shopping this week. Once again she came dangerously close to overdrawing the account. Good thing supermarkets now take charge cards, she thought.

Recently I taught macroeconomics for the first time, giving me an opportunity to more thoroughly study the prosperity and perils of the U.S. economy at the close of the twentieth century. By most accounts, the 1990s were a financial windfall for the world's richest nation. Except for a recession at its beginning, the decade provided a wonderful combination of continuous economic growth and low inflation.

In the midst of all this prosperity, the 1990s saw the national savings rate fall to a negative level, meaning that we are collectively spending more than we earn each year. Given that information, it wouldn't be surprising to discover that bankruptcy rates have greatly exceeded levels experienced during the Great Depression. The richest nation in human history has put Ecclesiastes 5:10 to the test and proved it true: "Whoever loves money never has money enough; whoever loves wealth is never satisfied with his income."

The strange thing is that we Americans have been so wrapped up in our materialism for so long that we don't realize how greedy we have become. Anyone who has traveled much in the world is bound to notice the excessive nature of the American economy. This hit home with me when a Korean family we know quite well visited us in Maine. Our house, purchased less than a year before, had a finished basement, meaning we had, for the first time, a second bathroom, plus a spare bedroom for our frequent houseguests. I remember their daughter politely asking me why we had all those extra rooms in the house. Just months earlier I had patted myself on the back for showing restraint and buying a fairly average house by U.S. standards. For most of the world, however, a house that contains more rooms than people is extravagant.

No Rest for the Materialist

What does living in a rich nation have to do with rest? Quite a bit, actually. First of all, a materialistic lifestyle takes considerably more time to maintain than a simpler existence. Having more stuff means more time spent acquiring, maintaining, and replacing. For example, Americans are said to spend three to four times as many hours a year shopping as do people in Western Europe. We have so many shopping malls that they could hold the entire U.S. population at one time with room to spare. [1]

Having more stuff also tends to involve more worries and hassles. Who tends to worry more about vehicle damage or theft: the owner of a shiny, new Mercedes or the driver of a ten-year-old Ford Escort? One of the biggest worries involved with out-of-control materialism is the growing debt burden that almost inevitably follows. The story of Janet paying her bills would have been considered a gross exaggeration twenty years ago. Today, her plight is commonplace, for the average balance of the 50 million households carrying credit card debt is $7,000 and growing. [2]

These days, an acquisition-oriented household can rarely have its material demands paid for by one person working a forty-hour week. In many families, both parents work outside the home, not for personal fulfillment or social interaction, but because two incomes are necessary to keep up with all the bills. Also, most highly paid professions are noted for long working hours. Aspiring physicians and lawyers are practically worked to death by their superiors in order to "pay their dues." Fast-track companies expect any ambitious salaried employees to put in sixty- to eighty-hour weeks. Few people accidentally make a lot of money. It usually requires a total commitment of a person's time, often leaving him or her too tired to have a real life outside of work.

The final blow of materialism to our quest for rest is lack of contentment. So far in my life, I have met only a handful of people I would describe as truly content. Not one of them lives an affluent lifestyle. People wrapped up in their wealth have placed their trust in something that cannot bring deep satisfaction, plus it tends to draw them away from relationships with God and loved ones—the real sources of contentment. Henry David Thoreau wrote, "Superfluous wealth can buy superfluities only. Money is not required to buy one necessity of the soul." [3]

I must admit that part of the reason I treat the materialism of our culture so harshly is due to my own struggle to overcome it. It would be impossible to calculate the number of hours in my life that have been spent in shopping malls or leafing through mail-order catalogs. It took years for me to gain control of my purchases of clothing, books, and musical recordings. Despite my progress, you could still lock me in my house for more than a year without my running short of reading material, plus I could listen to a different recording each day. Although I try to live modestly, I am still more influenced by materialism than I like to admit.

Bible Warnings about Money

What little Bible teaching I hear on money these days can be summarized in one sentence: it is okay to have lots of money and things, just as long as you don't love them. Although the statement is true in some respects, it is not a very accurate summary of what the Bible says about wealth. Money is more than just a good thing that can be abused. It has great potential to corrupt the heart and soul, which is why the Bible contains frequent warnings about its dangers.

Jesus taught volumes about money, both with His words and His lifestyle. The short version is this: Our attitudes toward money are indicative of how we have responded to God's invitation to have a relationship with Him through His Son, Jesus Christ. If we choose to love and follow Jesus, our focus will be on Him, His teachings, and storing up "treasures in heaven" through good works of love. If we choose to love and follow the world, our focus will be on ourselves, on acquiring money and possessions, on building up "treasures on earth." In Matthew 6:19-24, Jesus made it clear that we can have only one love, one master. What kind of treasures we are storing up—heavenly or earthly—is an indication of whether God or self is the ruler of our hearts. "For where your treasure is, there your heart will be also" (verse 21).

Jesus pointed out that no one can serve two masters and went on to name them: "You cannot serve both God and Money" (verse 24). The two are mutually exclusive love pursuits, much like a fork in the road that forces us to choose one route over another. Money has its uses, but when we make it our master, it puts us on a dangerous path. First Timothy 6:10 states that "the love of money is a root of all kinds of evil." If you look closely at all of the evil in the world, you will find greed at the heart of much of it.

Jesus did not attach much importance to worldly wealth. After warning a crowd about greed, Jesus said in Luke 12:15, "A man's life does not consist in the abundance of his possessions." The world may gauge a person's worth in terms of his or her wealth, but God does not. Jesus lived the most successful life in history, yet He did not appear to own anything more than the clothes on His back. Could Jesus have been rich? Certainly the attainment of wealth was in His power, but He did not pursue it. He had more important matters to attend to. As His followers, so do we.

Christians in the United States are some of the busiest, weariest people I've seen, largely because they are trying to pursue the things of God on top of the pursuits of the world. Doing one of these is hard enough; doing both is impossible. Remember this: you can't do it all! It is folly to assume we can grow in our faith, actively serve God and our church, raise perfect families, create showplace homes, rise to the top of our professions, own and use all the latest technological gadgets, achieve financial independence, and be seen as pillars of the community. If we push to achieve all these things we will either fail in several areas or wear ourselves out trying to succeed.

Instead, God wants us to pursue Him alone. Then He'll provide what we need and guide us in what we need to do. As we grow in our faith, we will discover that much of what we thought we needed no longer holds our interest. Following God does not require us to take a vow of poverty, but we do need to break free of our bondage to the love of money.

Do I Love Money?

This question is an important one for all of us to address periodically, given that Jesus teaches that we cannot love both God and money. In order to follow the command to "keep your lives free from the love of money" found in Hebrews 13:5, it is helpful to figure out what such love entails. Although no formal test exists to prove our love for money, the following questions may provide some indication as to our susceptibility to its wiles.

• **Do I strongly desire to be rich?** "Who doesn't want to be rich?" you ask. Well, love and desire are closely related emotions. The Bible condemns such desires, noting in Proverbs 28:20 that "one eager to get rich will not go unpunished." According to 1 Timothy 6:10, wanting to get rich can have dangerous consequences. "Some people, eager for money, have wandered from the faith and pierced themselves with many griefs." Wanting to earn a living is one thing, but an eagerness for riches is another.

• **How do I feel when my possessions get lost, stolen, or broken?** It is easy to get angry or hurt when we lose our nice possessions. However, when we can't get the loss off our minds or it affects our relationships with others, our possessions may have grown too close to our hearts. We need to quickly purge ourselves of any outrage when toddlers break the good china, teenagers total the family car, thieves clean out the garage, or stores won't give refunds on now-broken purchases. In Luke 6:30 Jesus instructs us "if anyone takes what belongs to you, do not demand it back." If we see money and possessions as loans from God instead of "mine," we won't get nearly as upset when we no longer have them.

• **How much do acquiring and managing wealth figure into my life goals?** Although God wants us to be good stewards of the material blessings He gives us, lovers of money are often obsessed with their financial portfolios. Most of their goals pertain to income and financial worth, providing an accurate picture of where their treasures lie. Before he became a Christian, entrepreneur Jerry Dettinger had a goal to become a millionaire by age thirty. After he accepted Christ, he said that net worth was "not a driving force in my life anymore."

• **Have disputes over money or possessions damaged any of my relationships with others?** When a person's money becomes more important to him than relationships, that person clearly loves money. Of course, few will say they value money more than people, but people act that way all the time. Conflicts about money are a primary or contributing factor in the breakup of many marriages. Disputes over the distribution of estates cause countless families to be ripped apart instead of coming together in their time of grief. Neighbors may refuse to speak to one another because one does something that negatively affects the property value of the other. We need to remember that in God's eyes, people are infinitely more important than wealth or possessions.

• **Do I take pride in my possessions and/or desire compliments from others?** Although we should be grateful to God for all He provides, we often turn our focus toward keeping up with and impressing others. Are our homes comfortable and set up for family convenience or are they showplaces filled with all the right niceties to create good impressions? Do we take great pride in our possessions or the "great deals" we got in purchasing them? Sometimes in our efforts to get by with less, we become slaves to sales, coupons, and comparison shopping. I've long been a clearance-rack clothing shopper and every time someone compliments me on the clothing I purchased, I fight the temptation to try to impress them with my shopping prowess by telling how little I paid for the items.

• **How easily do I give money and things away?** Money loses its hold on us when we give it away. Yet generous giving is difficult if we haven't finished acquiring all that we desire. In the world's wealthiest nation, only 5 percent of the population gives a tithe (10 percent or more) to their church. The average giver at church contributes just 2 percent of his or her income. [4] This lack of giving indicates that we are stifling God's work by our own greed. It is also a telling sign of where our hearts lie. According to 1 John 3:17, "If anyone has material possessions and sees his brother in need but has no pity on him, how can the love of God be in him?"

• **Do I spend more time shopping or praying?** This is admittedly a question that oversimplifies the materialism issue. Still, it can provide some insight into which kind of treasures we are currently storing up. Where do our hearts lie if we spend an hour or more each evening paging through mail-order catalogs or shopping on the Internet, yet can't spare a few minutes for Bible reading or prayer? What does it mean if we spend the bulk of our weekends at the mall, yet can't find time for church?

• **Do I frequently worry about money or possessions?** When people fully trust in God, their worries are infrequent and don't last long. Those who place their trust in things are plagued with worry. How do I make more money? What if I get robbed? What if the stock market crashes? What if I lose my job? Will I have enough money to live comfortably throughout my life? There is no rest for the worried wealthy.

• **Is my overall level of debt increasing or decreasing each year?** Some circumstances make it difficult to spend less than you earn, such as going to college or being unemployed. Also, the purchase of your first house is almost certain to increase your level of debt. Except for those kinds of situations, our household debt should be going down as the years go by. When we chronically spend more than we make, we are telling God through our actions that His financial blessings are inadequate. When the richest nation in history can't collectively live within its massive income, it is a clear sign that our love for money has run amuck.

• **How much time, effort, or money do I devote to "easy money" schemes?** Those who love money and desire more of it are easy prey for those who promise a quick path to riches. Such get-rich-quick schemes are almost too numerous to list: lotteries, gambling, big-money contests, most multilevel or network marketing organizations, amateur stock market day-trading, and the money-making opportunities featured on TV infomercials and the like. Of course the odds of making substantial amounts of easy money through any of these approaches is astronomical. Still, millions of people waste time and money pursuing their cherished dreams of financial independence, despite the fact that their efforts are likely to make them worse off in the long run. If the people who spend $20 a week for lottery tickets would put the money in mutual funds, they would be trading an unattainable fantasy for the reality of financial security.

• **If I never acquired another thing or made more money than I do today, would I be content with what I have?** Since the Bible says that those who love money never have enough, contentment is strong evidence of Christ's unrivaled rule in our hearts. Paul writes in 1 Timothy 6:6 that "godliness with contentment is great gain." However, if contentment is always a goal to be reached after the next car purchase or promotion, our message to God is that His current provision for us is not good enough. The desire for "one more thing" is far more dangerous than it appears. First, it puts our attention on what we lack, making it more difficult to enjoy what we have. Also, as soon as we attain that "one more thing," another thing always, I repeat always, pops up to take its place.

Ways to Step Back from the Material World

How do we stay clear of the love of money that steals our love for God and robs us of rest? Becoming less money-oriented doesn't require taking a vow of poverty, but rather gaining a distance or detachment from our possessions. We step back from the material world, not because things are inherently bad, but because we can get so attached to them that we choose them over our relationships to God and others. To step back from the material world is to become less things-centered and more relationship-centered. Lessening your materialistic pursuits will also free up some slack in your schedule for rest and greater enjoyment of what you now have. Here are some ways to help you take that step.

• **Practice tithing.** Gordon MacDonald writes that, just as God provides us with the Sabbath as a hedge against workaholism, He also prescribes the tithe as protection against materialism. "It is virtually impossible for a person to become an obsessive hoarder of material things when the tithe is built in as a discipline." [5] Want to free yourself from the love of money? Start giving away at least 10 percent of every bit of money you earn. People who regularly give back to God His share of what they earn almost never stop the practice, because the spiritual blessings far outweigh the financial cost.

• **Give away or get rid of some of your stuff.** To go through your possessions and thin them out has two benefits. First, the act of giving away stuff helps rid us of our attachment to things. Having fewer things also reduces the stress of having more possessions than we can possibly use at once. "Sell your possessions and give to the poor, and you will have treasure in heaven" was the command Jesus gave to the rich young man in Matthew 19:21. One way to fulfill the intent of that verse is to hold a garage or yard sale for a cause. One small group we belonged to held a garage sale to help support the moving expenses of a family going out to the mission field. Another approach is to simply bring a carload of clothing and household items to the Salvation Army. It is a quick and painless way to reduce the clutter and feel good at the same time.

• **Set limits for yourself in areas of spending temptation.** As I mentioned before, my main shopping weaknesses have been in the areas of clothing, books, and musical recordings. I still set an annual limit to the amount of money I spend on clothes and the number of books I buy. It keeps down the clutter, helps balance the family budget, and reduces the time I spend shopping. If you face spending temptations wherever you turn, try a month-long shopping fast—that is, do no shopping of any sort (unless you can't get another family member to buy groceries). Once you place some limits on your material desires, they begin to lose their hold on you.

• **Put a dent in your debt.** If your level of personal debt has been regularly rising, make a commitment to live within your income for the coming year. Once you have succeeded in ending the accumulation of debt, it is time to set aside some money each month to begin paying off your debts. For most families, the best place to start is to pay down any credit card balances. Investment expert Andrew Tobias writes that paying off your credit card balance "is just about the best 'investment' you can ever make." [6] One place to contact for more resources to help you in your financial planning is Christian Financial Concepts (P.O. Box 2377, Gainesville, GA 30503-2377, www.cfcministry.org).

• **Delay and pray before you pay.** Many financial counselors recommend always making a list before you go shopping to minimize impulse buying. My advice is to take it a step further. Make your list at least a day in advance and pray to God to give you wisdom in sorting out what you truly need. I find this particularly helpful with mail-order catalogs. A couple months ago, I received a tea catalog and convinced myself I "needed" a cast-iron teapot, plus a large order of teas to add to my already well-stocked shelf. If I had ordered without delay, I would be at least $100 poorer. Someday I might actually get around to ordering some tea, but buying a third teapot is not on my list any longer.

• **Share your "toys" with others.** Somehow we have gotten the impression that every household must be self-sufficient. We must have on hand every tool, appliance, and recreational toy we could ever think of using. Does everyone with a large garden need a rototiller, even though it is used only once a year? Anything we own that is infrequently used could probably be shared with several other families. According to Dietrich Bonhoeffer, "Earthly goods are given to be used, not to be collected. . . . Hoarding is idolatry." [7] Churches could also help encourage such material sharing, since it increases what people can use and enjoy while lessening their financial burdens. For example, Kathy and I are able to enjoy swimming on a hot day or a crackling fire in an outdoor gazebo without owning either because we have friends who are generous with their possessions.

- **Learn to want and enjoy what you have right now.** Instead of spending your time thinking about what you'd like to have, a more restful approach is to focus on enjoying what you have right now. This is much easier to explain than to do. When I feel envious of the man driving a new BMW convertible, I should instead be thankful that I own a dependable vehicle that doesn't require monthly loan or lease payments (something I couldn't say if I owned the BMW). Instead of wishing for an office with a panoramic view, I need to look up from my computer screen to the hummingbird feeder less than ten feet away, where I can gaze at one of God's most magnificent creatures. When we can regularly focus on our blessings instead of what we lack, we have taken a giant step back from the allure of the material world.

Next Step

Take a few minutes to review your current financial situation. Are material woes robbing you of rest? Pick out one thing you could start doing this week to help relieve some of your financial stress. Perhaps it would be to delay or forgo making a major purchase. Or to give away some of your clutter of possessions. Or lock up your credit cards for a few months. Don't underestimate the rest value of dematerializing your life. Billy Graham once said, "If a person gets his attitude toward money straight, it will help straighten out almost every other area of his life."

Notes:

1. Juliet B. Schor, *The Overworked American* (New York: BasicBooks, 1991), p. 107.

2. Andrew Tobias, "Take Control of Your Credit Cards," *Parade Magazine*, November 1, 1998, p. 4.

3. Henry David Thoreau, *Walden and Other Writings* (New York: Bantam Books, 1962), p. 347.

4. George Barna, *The Index of Leading Spiritual Indicators* (Dallas: Word Publishing, 1996), p. 111.

5. Gordon MacDonald, *Restoring Your Spiritual Passion* (Nashville: Thomas Nelson Publishers, 1986), p. 165.

6. Andrew Tobias, "Take Control of Your Credit Cards," *Parade* Magazine, November 1, 1998, p. 4.

7. Dietrich Bonhoeffer, *The Cost of Discipleship* (New York: Macmillan Publishing Company, 1963), p. 194.

Chapter 16

Conclusion: The Rewards of Rest

The doors to Rapid Technology, Inc. opened and a steady stream of workers shuffled in to begin a new week of work. As they reached their desks and workstations, an audible groan could be heard throughout the building. They were greeted by another urgent request from a major client that needed to be handled by noon. All employees would need to drop everything and work at a frenzied pace to meet the deadline. For this organization, it was just a typical Monday morning.

Peter casually strolled into this chaotic scene, whistling a tune he had practiced on the piano over the weekend. He smiled and waved as he passed by fast-moving coworkers, many already looking stressed-out after just a few minutes of work.

He stopped by the coffeepot nearest his office, where a small gathering of colleagues were waking up and comparing notes. "Good morning! Did everyone have a great weekend?"

"Well, Peter obviously hasn't seen the memo on his desk yet," said Jack, a fellow manager. "Here, take a look at my copy."

Peter scanned the memo and smiled, gently shaking his head. "At least I *won't have trouble deciding what to work on today."*

Dawn stared at him as she sipped her coffee. "You're taking it awfully well. How are we supposed to get all this done?"

"I agree, they should've given us more time for this. Still, if we pull together and don't panic, we'll make it. We've done it before."

"Peter, why is it that you stay so calm, no matter how crazy it gets around here?" Dawn asked. "I can't understand it. You work at least as hard as the rest of us and yet you always seem to be at peace with the world. How do you do it? What's your secret?"

What a wonderful opportunity Peter has here to share his faith. Wouldn't spreading the Good News of Jesus Christ be so much easier if people came to us and asked us to share our secret?

Peter's workplace behavior demonstrates the principle of being a witness for Christ. The Bible does not call us to "do" witnessing but to "be" witnesses. We are to give people a glimpse of Jesus in who we are and how we live. Then, and only then, will they want to hear us talk about a relationship with Jesus. They might even bring the subject up.

Ultimately, finding rest is not just about gaining a little sanity in a stressed-out world. When we enter into a relationship with Jesus Christ, we obtain the promise of rest both here and throughout eternity—but that's just for starters. God also allows us the honor of participating in His ministry of drawing all people to Himself, a task we undertake in cooperation with other believers who make up the body of Christ, His church.

So how does rest relate to that work? Since finding real rest involves finding God, the peace that comes from a growing faith relationship becomes an outward sign that others will notice. People who are calm in the face of crises will stand out. Those who are content, with no need to prove anything to anyone, will attract attention. Men and women who face future uncertainties without worry will cause people to wonder. In short, a rested, growing Christian can be one of God's most powerful tools for reaching a frantic, yet weary, world. Imagine how God can use believers with time in their schedules to respond to people in need, mental energy to offer wise counsel at the end of a long day, emotional reserves to get involved and lift up others in their struggles, and a closeness to God that allows the Holy Spirit to provide strength and direction.

The Fundamentals of Rest

How do we become the kind of person that God can mightily use to reach a restless world? The purpose of this book has been to explain a biblical approach to bringing about this kind of change. I would like to conclude by summarizing some of the key rest practices I have advocated throughout the book.

• **Make Jesus your Lord and following Him your focus.** Until you discover the rest for the soul Jesus promises to those who come to Him, all other rest practices offer little more than a brief interruption from life's stresses. This commitment to Jesus is more involved than merely going to church or saying "yes" to Jesus to avoid going to hell. Having Jesus rule your heart is a radically different way of living, one that will forever change your life. If you are ready to receive God's rest, you might want to turn back to the "Next Step" portion of chapter 7.

• **Develop a meaningful daily time of prayer and Bible reading.** Experiencing the stillness and quiet of God's presence on a daily basis is one of the most powerful rest practices available. First thing in the morning or late at night are times that seem to hold the best potential for quiet in most households. Find a comfortable place where you can be alone for at least a half hour to an hour. Focus more on being still and sensing His presence and less on what you are going to say.

• **Create a Sabbath day of rest every week.** For an increasing number of people, day-to-day life is like one continuous run on a treadmill. To avoid wearing out, it is critical for all of us to hop off the treadmill at least one day each week to experience living at a more leisurely pace. For much of my life I have labored to achieve lofty ambitions and have periodically experienced varying degrees of burnout. Since I have developed the weekly discipline of Sabbath rest, those stressful stretches of time that used to wear me out no longer have the same impact. It is

189

a practice that has given me a new approach to work. These days I am much too busy to spend every day working.

• **Go on a personal retreat at least once a year.** Periodically, we all need the opportunity to get away for a few days of quiet reflection and prayer. While daily prayer and the Sabbath strengthen us for day-to-day activities, retreats help us determine lifelong goals and changes of direction. Without those regular times to get away, my life and work would not even remotely resemble what they do today.

• **Average at least eight hours of sleep a night.** Despite the obvious health benefits, this is one rest practice I have yet to fully achieve. Although I have progressed from my years of six-hour sleeping, I am still struggling to average eight hours for a full week or more. In my quest for more sleep, I have been unsuccessful in sleeping in much later. I top eight hours only when I force myself to go to bed earlier at night. Even though I have yet to feel the full effects of getting more sleep, I can assure you there is no truth to the saying, "You snooze, you lose." The more I sleep, the more I seem to get done.

• **Trust God by turning your worries over to Him each day.** Finding rest today is difficult when we are filled with anxiety about the future. Only God can control the future, so we need to demonstrate our trust in Him by turning over our worries. Jesus taught us not to worry about tomorrow because God will take care of us—and because each day has enough troubles without adding more to it. Our responsibility is to do our best each day and leave the results in God's capable and caring hands.

• **Hold no grudges.** We all get angry from time to time, but sustained anger robs us of rest. The advice of Ephesians 4:26 to "not let the sun go down while you are still angry" is sound. Regardless of whether we are right or wrong in the situation, any time we lose control of our anger, we need to apologize. Whenever we are wronged, we need to be quick to forgive, just as God is always quick to forgive our own transgressions.

• **Make a point each day to count your blessings, not your problems.**
This act of being thankful is one of the best methods I know of developing contentment. God accepts us just as we are, so we need to do the same of ourselves (and of all those other people God also loves). Whatever situations we face, we need to accept that God is working in them for our ultimate best interest. When thanksgiving is practiced every day instead of just on Thanksgiving Day, we will begin to see each new morning as a glorious gift from God.

Next Step

Review the list of rest fundamentals and select one to be your emphasis for the coming month. I pray that God might bless you in your efforts.

Appendix

Questions for Group Discussion

I f you are interested in using *Finding Rest When the Work Is Never Done* in a small group or classroom setting, the following questions are included as a resource for generating meaningful discussion. Although each teacher has his or her own style, one approach for discussing each chapter is to:

• Give a brief overview of chapter content. Ask if anyone has any questions about the chapter or needs clarification.

• Go through the discussion questions, relating back to chapter content as necessary.

• Ask people to volunteer responses to the "Next Step" application activity at the end of the chapter.

• Discuss additional ways to apply the material in the chapter to day-to-day living.

Chapter 1: Is It Normal to Be So Tired?

1. What comes to mind when you think of the term *rest?*
2. Would rest generally be considered an important activity by those in our culture? Why or why not?
3. Which of the attitudes toward rest listed in the chapter best fits with your own view of rest? Why do you feel that way about rest?
4. What are the dangers or drawbacks to working too hard and not getting enough rest? Have any of you experienced some of the consequences of not resting listed in the chapter?

Chapter 2: Created for Both Work and Rest

1. What are some of the reasons why many of us work too much and rest too little?
2. Why does God want us to rest? Do most people follow the Old Testament passages listed in the chapter commanding rest? Why or why not?
3. What are some of the cultural trends that make rest more difficult to achieve?
4. Read Exodus 20:8-11. In what ways do we break this commandment today? How would you compare the importance of this commandment to the other nine?
5. How does restlessness relate to sin?
6. Why do most of us value work more than rest? Do the Bible passages cited in this chapter suggest our priorities might be off-target?

Chapter 3: A Body That Will Quit

1. List some ways that we can love the Lord our God with all our heart, soul, mind, and strength.
2. What kinds of damage can chronic stress do to our bodies? If most people were aware of the potential damage, do you think they would get more rest? Why or why not?
3. Why are people sleeping less in our culture? What are some of the dangers of getting too little sleep?
4. Read 1 Corinthians 6:19-20. How might thinking of our bodies as temples of the Holy Spirit change the way we look at them? At how we take care of them?

5. Read Hebrews 12:1. How might we follow its instructions to "run with perseverance the race marked out for us"?

Chapter 4: A Mind at Rest

1. How many of you agree with the statement, "I can't imagine ever just sitting around doing nothing"? Why are we so opposed to being "still" as the Bible commands?
2. What are some of the reasons why people can't stop their endless cycle of activity?
3. What kinds of things do we worry about? Do most of the things we worry about actually happen? Does worrying do anything to help out our situations?
4. Why does the Bible repeatedly instruct us not to worry? If we love and trust God, do we have any cause to worry?
5. Read Philippians 4:6-7. What are we to do with our anxieties? Have any of you experienced the peace that comes from taking your anxieties to the Lord? Have one or more class members share their experiences.
6. Read Luke 10:38-42. Which of the women do you relate to better: Mary or Martha? What are some ways we can focus on what is important (like Mary) and worry less (like Martha)?

Chapter 5: A Heart Full of Contentment

1. With what kinds of things in our lives do we tend to become dissatisfied?
2. How can our expectations affect our level of satisfaction and contentment?
3. How does comparing our situation with others affect our level of contentment and rest?
4. In what ways can we cultivate more contentment in our lives?
5. List some of the many things you/we have to be thankful for.

Chapter 6: A Soul Resting in Jesus

1. How does the emptiness many people feel relate to the restlessness of our culture?
2. Read Psalm 62:1-2. How does God act as our "rock" and our "fortress?"

3. Read Psalm 23. How does God act as our shepherd? How might this provide us more rest and less of the emptiness the rest of the world feels?
4. Have each member of the group rate him- or herself on a scale of one to ten (one being miserable, ten being great) for each category of rest: body, mind, heart, soul. Then compare individual scores to see similarities and differences. As a group, which area of rest needs the most work?

Chapter 7: Enter God's Rest
1. Read Matthew 11:28-30. What do you think Jesus means when He asks us to "come" to Him? How does that bring us rest for our souls?
2. Jesus promises us a light burden. If God does not lay heavy burdens on us, then where do they come from? For what reasons do people carry around their heavy burdens and ignore the promise of relief Jesus gives?
3. Read John 14:27. Jesus promises to give us His peace. What do you think He means when He says, "I do not give to you as the world gives"?
4. Look at Rest Benefit number 8. How does guilt rob us of rest? How does having a relationship with Jesus address this problem?

Chapter 8: Schedule Your Life with Purpose
1. What kind of important activities do we frequently put off because they have no time urgency to them? If we were able to do these things more regularly, how would our lives be better?
2. To understand God's priorities, read Mark 12:30-31 and Matthew 28:18-20. What activities, both individually and as a church, might fall under these commands?
3. Devote class time to letting people individually work through the five steps identified in the chapter. Give them a simple example to work with as a guide. Ask for volunteers to share what they discovered. In addition to or in place of this exercise, you could have each person spend a few minutes pondering the question: What one additional thing could I do that would make the greatest difference in my personal or professional life? Again, ask for volunteers to share their answers.

Chapter 9: Find Your Daily Rest in Jesus

1. Review the rest benefits of a relationship with Jesus from chapter 8. What are some reasons why we might not be experiencing all those benefits?
2. Think about the people with whom you have the closest relationships. What are some of the requirements for building a strong relationship? Which of these requirements also fit in building a strong relationship with Jesus?
3. How many of you sometimes struggle to find enough time to pray? What kinds of things keep us from spending time with God?
4. In what ways can daily prayer provide us with rest?
5. You may want to spend some time in prayer as a group. One approach is to pray through the various aspects of prayer presented in the chapter. Another approach is to have several minutes of silent prayer or silent meditation on a particular passage of Scripture.

Chapter 10: Rediscover the Sabbath

1. Why is Sabbath rest so important, according to the Bible?
2. What are the biblical requirements for the Sabbath?
3. What are some of the reasons Sabbath rest is ignored or poorly followed by so many of us?
4. In Mark 2:27, Jesus said, "The Sabbath was made for man, not man for the Sabbath." What implications does that statement have for how we practice the Sabbath and how we encourage others to practice it?
5. What kinds of things might we do on the Sabbath? Make a list of potential options.

Chapter 11: Restore Rest through Retreat

1. How does the retreat described in the chapter differ from church or business retreats?
2. What may be some of the benefits of going on a rest-oriented retreat?
3. What are some of the reasons we might put off scheduling an extended period of time with God? Are there some ways these barriers can be overcome?
4. See if anyone in your group has been on a retreat similar to the ones

described in the chapter. Ask him or her to share the experience.

5. Ask to see if there is any interest in your group or class to experience such a retreat together.

Chapter 12: Keep a Constant Eye on the Fuel Gauge

1. What are some of the reasons people let their own "fuel gauges" run to empty?
2. What signs might indicate that our own fuel gauges might be nearing empty, leading us to burnout?
3. What kinds of experiences tend to drain us of energy?
4. What practices help us to restore lost energy?
5. How can we best ensure that our fuel gauges stay well above empty?

Chapter 13: Learn to Forgive and Forget

1. In what ways do conflict and anger rob us of rest?
2. Why is it sometimes difficult to forgive those who wrong us?
3. Is forgiving others an option, according to God? What are the consequences of not forgiving others?
4. What does the Bible say about forgiving repeat offenders?
5. How can we live out the kind of love that "keeps no record of wrongs," according to 1 Corinthians 13?

Chapter 14: Creating Rest Where You Live, Work, and Worship

1. How do other people and the environments around us affect our ability to find more rest?
2. What are some ways we can create more rest in our households?
3. What are some characteristics of a sane work environment?
4. How can churches help keep their pastors from burning out?
5. In what ways can churches help create a more restful environment for all their people?

Chapter 15: Step Back from the Material World

1. How can material possessions and riches rob us of rest?
2. What kind of dangers does the Bible point out regarding money?

3. Read 1Timothy 6:9-10. What kind of temptations and grief can the love of money lead to?

4. What are some indicators that we might be susceptible to the love of money?

5. What steps can we take to better keep our possessions from possessing us?

Chapter 16: Conclusion: The Rewards of Rest

1. How can a rested Christian be of more use to God than a stressed-out Christian?

2. What concepts presented in this book have been most useful to you in your life?

3. Has anyone begun to adopt any of the rest practices presented here?

4. Have you noticed any benefits so far?

5. How can the members of this class/group help one another implement these practices?

6. Can you think of topics presented in this book that you would like this group to study in greater depth?

About the Author

Patrick Klingaman is founder and president of Meaningful Work & Leisure, which provides resources to help people find more meaning and spiritual significance in their lives and in their work. He is a speaker to both business and Christian groups, besides teaching business courses at area colleges. He is also author of the book *Thank God It's Monday: Making Business Your Ministry*. Patrick and his wife, Kathy, live in Wells, Maine.

If you would like information on scheduling Patrick as a speaker or would like a free copy of his *Meaningful Work & Leisure* newsletter, you can write to him at one of the addresses listed below. If you made a decision to commit your life to Jesus during the course of reading this book, Patrick will send or e-mail you a free short report, "Growing in Jesus," if you drop him a line.

Patrick Klingaman, Meaningful Work & Leisure, 21 Davis St., Wells, ME 04090

E-mail address: klingaman@cybertours.com (Original messages only, please. Any forwarded or "chain" messages will be returned unread.)